Comprehensive Security
Challenge for Pacific Asia

James C. Hsiung
New York University

UNIVERSITY OF INDIANAPOLIS PRESS

2004

Planning: Phylis Lan Lin, Executive Director, University of Indianapolis Press

Cover design and layout: Jeannine Allen
Editors: David Noble, Peter Noot, Erling Peterson, Stephanie Seifert

University of Indianapolis Press Advisory Board (2003-2005):
Shirley Bigna, Phylis Lan Lin, David Noble, Peter Noot, Philip Young

Printed in the United States of America

09 08 07 06 05 04   10 9 8 7 6 5 4 3 2 1

ISBN: 0-880938-56-0

Published by
University of Indianapolis Press
University of Indianapolis
1400 East Hanna Avenue
Indianapolis, IN 46227-3697

Fax: (317) 788-3480
E-mail: lin@uindy.edu
http://www.uindy.edu/universitypress

ABSTRACT

This study identifies the origin, components, and significance of comprehensive security (CS) and uses Pacific Asia (in this study, denoting what is usually known as Asia Pacific minus North America) as an illustration of CS's practical implications and challenges for policy responses as well as our conceptualization about security studies. The study begins with a comparison of CS with traditional security (national defense), both in its concerns and scope. It also notes two commonalities that CS shares with the post-9/11 modified traditional notion of security (antiterrorism). Applying the CS perspective to Pacific Asia, this study finds that Pacific Asia's longest suit is in the area of economic security; its record in human security is spotty; and environmental security is the region's Achilles' heel. Many of the problems in the latter category, such as increasing terrorism and maritime piracy, not to mention the threats of sea-level rises as a result of global warming, would require collaborative solutions beyond the reach of any single nation. The essay ends with a speculation on the likelihood of these collaborative efforts.

CONTENTS

RISE OF COMPREHENSIVE SECURITY

A burning issue on the agenda of nations in the twenty-first century is the new meaning of security and its place in world politics. A nation's security is no longer the traditional "national defense" (military security) but has economic, environmental, and human dimensions as well (separately known as economic security, environmental security, and human security). All three dimensions may be subsumed under the rubric of "comprehensive security," a new umbrella concept that grew out of the post-Cold War debate over the ramifications of security and over security studies as a field of inquiry.[1] Olaf Palme, the late Swedish prime minister who headed the Commission on Disarmament and Security Issues created in 1981, is sometimes credited with having been the first to advance the notion of "comprehensive security."[2] The exact import of the concept, however, has varied and expanded over time. The Commission, which appropriated Palme's name, developed the idea of mutual security, to be achieved through cooperation, as no country could win a nuclear war, and it argued against reliance on nuclear deterrence.[3] Other writers, using the same concept, gave mutual security quite different meanings. One writer, for example, invoking Japanese Prime Minister Masayoshi Ohira's idea of comprehensive security, lists the following requirements: a vibrant industrial base, a robust economy, beneficial export relationships, and an active foreign assistance program.[4] In this view, comprehensive security entails the protection of these vital ingredients.

Comprehensive security is not just a fashionable buzzword for academics and armchair strategists. It has entered the conscious policy-planning of government security managers in Washington, D.C., and other national capitals. In 1998 the Pentagon issued a report known as "U.S. Security Strategy for the East Asia-Pacific Region," which included a new section on "The Search for Comprehensive Security: Transnational Security

Challenges for the 21st Century" (emphasis added).[5] The governments of Japan and China, each in its own way, likewise turned their attentions to a similar search for comprehensive security.[6] In the Pentagon's usage, comprehensive security demands vigilance on a panoply of concerns such as terrorism, environmental degradation, infectious diseases, drug trafficking, energy, and humanitarian relief. For our discussions, these issues properly fall under the categories of environmental security and human security. And, in our usage, comprehensive security has a third component—economic security.

This essay presents a coherent exposition of the concept of comprehensive security and its significance for security studies. I shall first note its differences in conceptualization with traditional security and follow with a more in-depth discourse on the meanings of each of comprehensive security's three named components. In the final section, I shall turn to the challenge that confronts Pacific Asian nations in the age of comprehensive security, as the memories of the Asian financial crisis of the late 1990s (a breach of their economic security) and the recent SARS epidemic (an invasion of human security) still haunt many in the region. I hope this chosen regional focus will serve an illustrative purpose for other regions and will provide relevant insights for grappling with the new concept of comprehensive security.

COMPREHENSIVE SECURITY VERSUS THE TRADITIONAL NOTION OF SECURITY

Security has traditionally been defined in terms of states and the qualities of statehood. The "modern" science of security studies (in the traditional sense), as Steven Walt argues, has evolved around seeking "cumulative knowledge" about the role of military force.[7] Until the end of the Cold War, "national security," as it was known, always focused on the military defense of the state.[8] In contrast to comprehensive security, the traditional concept of national security embraces two distinct characteristics.[9] First, security is commensurate with national survival in a system of world politics that is inherently contentious and anarchical,[10] and the State is the central unit of analysis. Second, understanding force postures and capabilities is a key tenet of traditional security. Sovereign states develop military doctrines: weapons systems serve their defense but may also intensify interstate conflicts and fuel security dilemmas.[11] In short, in the anarchical Westphalian system we live in, security in the traditional sense can be simply defined as the absence of physical threat to the territorial and functional integrity of a state.[12] In this sense, all the antiterror concerns in a heightened-security-conscious world after September 11 are still largely within the traditional concept of security, as the term "homeland security" implies, although antiterrorism may have implications for human security as well.

Comprehensive security, by contrast, demonstrates two distinct shifts away from the state as the central unit of analysis, representing two opposite but ultimately interrelated foci. The first shift is toward focusing on the external community at large, as it has been shown that the rampaging forces of the environment and the ravaging effects of globalization go far beyond the ability of the state to contain them by its own resources. Epidemics like AIDS and the recent SARS attacks in East and Southeast Asia in early 2003 are but a potent reminder of this new reality. Another such reminder is the series of financial crises hitting Europe (early 1990s), Latin America (1994–1995), and Pacific Asia (1997–1999), leaving no nation unaffected in their trail.

The other trend is a shift inward from the state toward the individual citizen, in terms of human security. As defined by the United Nations Human Development Report of 1994, human security includes "safety from chronic threats such as hunger, disease, and repression, as well as protection from sudden and harmful disruptions in the patterns of daily life."[13] In the growing literature, the concept of human security has been expanded to include economic, health, and environmental concerns, as well as the physical security of the individual.[14] I might add that the post-9/11 atmosphere of ubiquitous terror, which threatens the peace of mind and quality of life of the ordinary individual, is a new source of sinister threat to human security, in addition to being a threat to a country's national security in the traditional sense.

The various components of comprehensive security are intertwined. Global warming may have worldwide economic implications, and epidemics may ravage the physical and economic security of the individual (and society at large). While seemingly heading in opposite directions, both the globalization shift and the opposite shift toward the individual are ultimately interrelated because the individual is the ultimate beneficiary of both environmental and economic security. In either case, the state loses its previous salience as the central focus and unit of analysis.

In the next section, I will discuss each of the three components of comprehensive security from a broad perspective.[15]

ECONOMIC SECURITY (GEOECONOMICS)

Recently, geoeconomics has risen to rival, even outweigh, geopolitics as a desideratum determining a country's national interest and its foreign policy behavior. This has come about not only because of the end of the Cold War but also, more importantly, because of the globalization of the world economy beyond the stage of complex interdependence. Although the term "geoeconomics" has been much bandied about, it needs a definition.[16] On the macro level, in the geoeconomic age, matters pertaining to manufacturing, marketing, financing, and research and development (R & D) are transnationalized and eventually globalized. On the micro level, national power is no longer measured exclusively, or even mainly, by a state's military might, and economic security has eclipsed, though not displaced, military security on the scales of strategic importance to a country's national interest. National power in this context is not only military might but also the aggregate of a number of components such as human and technological resources, exportable capital, efficient production of modern goods, influence over global economic decision making that affects one's own vital interests, and the will to mobilize economic capacity for national ends.[17]

This formulation, which combines both macro-level economic power management and micro-level implications for individual states caught in the shifting power game, captures the essence of geoeconomics as we use the term in this discourse. In addition to redefining power and what the new era's power configurations imply, the formulation also points up the paramountcy of geoeconomic calculations in the concerns of nations in world politics.

For an example of how geoeconomic desiderata may compound a country's foreign policy priorities, one need only recall Japan's response to the 1990–1991 Persian Gulf crisis, precipitated by Iraq's invasion and annexation of Kuwait. That event taught the Japanese a potent lesson on economic security and its geoeconomic imperative. The invasion exposed the vulnerability of the Japanese economy because of its total dependency on extra-regional supplies of vital resources. As the event woefully demonstrated, access to these supplies could be disrupted at any flare-up of a crisis in a far-off place, and Japan was at the mercy of forces beyond its control. Thus, while the world's industrial nations were carrying on the post-Tiananmen sanctions against Beijing, Japan began in the fall of 1990—during the height of the Gulf crisis—to switch gears and be the first industrial nation to return to China in a deliberate effort to uplift its ties with the Chinese, thus breaking ranks with the rest of G-7. It not only resumed bilateral trade but even extended to China US$54 billion in credits.[18]

Another instance demonstrating how the geoeconomic reflex held sway was the decision of the Hong Kong SAR government to intervene in the market in August 1998 during the course of the financial crisis hitting the Asian region. Although well-intentioned critics condemned the move as a betrayal of Hong Kong's long tradition of laissez-faire, the SAR government reacted in the same fashion as would any traditional government when its national security was breached by external military encroachments, considering the dictate of economic security in the age of geoeconomics.

As a caveat, I would reiterate for emphasis that geoeconomics have not replaced geopolitics. The competition between geopolitics and geoeconomics, in fact, offers an unavoidable complication to countries in figuring out their external friends and enemies. For instance, a foreign adversary in the geopolitical sense may very well be a great economic partner, such as in the case of China. Conversely, an ideologically defined ally like Japan may prove to be a potential economic rival, even a threat, despite its protracted economic downturn over a decade.[19]

ENVIRONMENTAL SECURITY (ECOPOLITICS)

Ecopolitics, strictly speaking, has a much broader connotation than the combination of the three terms—economics, ecology, and politics—of which the term is a contraction. In its original formulation by Dennis Pirages, global ecopolitics involves "the use of environment issues, control over natural resources, scarcity arguments, and related concerns of social justice to overturn the international hierarchical expansion."[20] Placing it in the context of human history, Pirages speaks of an ecopolitical revolution on a par with the two preceding human revolutions: the Agricultural Revolution (c. 8,000 B.C.) and the Industrial Revolution, which began in earnest in the eighteenth century and culminated in the rapid advance of technology that was characteristic of the twentieth century (p. 4). As such, the ecopolitical revolution encompasses a number of developments affecting all nations, subsumed under what Pirages calls a "new scarcity," resulting from the exponential growth of population. Ecopolitical revolution includes resource depletion, energy shortage, water shortage, and scarcity of food and nonfuel minerals, further compounded by a related issue—natural waste disposal (pp. 8-9). In our usage, "ecopolitics" refers to only the ecological and political dimensions of the concept because we discussed the economic component in the preceding section, in the context of geoeconomics, which was a term unknown when Pirages published his study.

Our concerns here are not merely with how environmental degradation affects the ecosystems, but also with the challenge it presents to nations in their mutual relations.[21] I wish to note that a dual linkage exists between international conflict and the environment. Disputes over control of shared resources (such as shared waters of international rivers) may lead to conflict while on the other hand renewal of resources (e.g., fish stocks) may be depleted as a result of conflict.

The threat of environmental degradation is far more serious than generally realized. Lester Brown has warned of the danger to humanity of climatic rise (global warming) as a result of increasing concentrations of carbon dioxide (CO_2), which had by 1998 hiked 131 percent in the two centuries since the Industrial Revolution. If CO_2 concentrations double preindustrial levels during the twenty-first century as projected, global temperature is expected to rise by at least one degree, and perhaps as much as four degrees, Celsius (or two to seven degrees Fahrenheit). Sea level is projected to rise from a minimum of seventeen centimeters to as much as one meter by 2100. As Brown summarizes, "this will alter every ecosystem on Earth."[22]

The modest but steady temperature rise in recent decades is already melting ice caps and glaciers. Ice cover is shrinking in the Arctic, the Antarctic, Greenland, the Alps, the Andes, and the Qinghai-Tibetan Plateau. If anyone still has doubts as to the long-term consequence of global warming, two recent bizarre incidents should serve as reminders. In the fall of 1991, hikers in the southwestern Alps near the border of Austria and Italy discovered an intact human body, a male, protruding from a glacier. The considerably well-preserved body was believed to have been trapped in a storm 5,000 years ago and quickly covered by snow and ice. Also, in the late summer of 1999, another body was found protruding from a melting glacier in Canada's Yukon territory. As Brown half-facetiously suggests, our ancestors are emerging from the ice with a message for us: Earth is getting too warm (p. 6)! His conclusion, however, is not frivolous: We should be "replacing economics with ecology" (pp. 8-10).

According to the latest reports, unusually high temperatures, drought, and forest fires brought suffering and death through the European continent and the British Isles in the summer of 2003. Preliminary estimates of farm losses alone rose to billions of dollars.[23] The news proved that global warming is not a problem limited only to any one particular or regional terrain. Considering the depleting fishery, forestry, and other resources, invoking the specter of global economic decline, and raising doubts as to the sustainability of global economic development, Brown's motto that we should be "replacing economics with ecology" (pp. 8-10) is a counsel of wisdom for all. In fact, the earliest official recognition of environmental hazards as a threat to national security probably went back to President George H. W. Bush. A 1991 presidential document summarizing the United States' national security objectives included "assuring the sustainability and environmental security of the planet . . . " (emphasis added).[24]

HUMAN SECURITY (HUMAN DEVELOPMENT)

Human security and human development fall into a continuum concerning human well-being. The former deals with the psychological end state of development instead of the more mechanical aspects of human development.[25] At a minimum, it is based on an individual and collective sense of protection from perceived present and potential threats to physical and psychological well-being from all manner of agents and forces affecting lives, values, and property.[26]

Human security is often subject to domestic structural conflict, or inequities of society (such as gross inequality in income distribution), and brute atrocities by the victims' own government, as has happened with increasing frequency in the past two decades in Rwanda and elsewhere. But these atrocities are not a monopoly of African nations. The Kosovo crisis dramatized the modern vulnerability of individuals to state aggression even in a European country.[27] Large-scale atrocities, crime, and terrorism, such as in the "ethnic cleansing" conducted by the self-designated central government in the disintegrating Yugoslavia, committed by governments against their own people were shocking to human conscience but also testified that brute violations of human security are not exclusively a third-world problem.

Although state terrorism is the most shocking and outrageous assault on the sanctity of human security, other less dramatic, although no less disconcerting, sources of human insecurity exist, such as:[28]

Income inequality,
Clean water shortage,
Illiteracy,
Food shortage,
Housing shortage, and
Infectious diseases.

Infectious diseases, especially, are a devastating scourge for Africa. A reported 23 million people in sub-Sahara Africa were said to have begun the twenty-first century with a death sentence imposed by HIV, the virus that leads to AIDS. For the first time in the modern era, life expectancy for an entire region is declining—threatening the economic future of 800 million people in sub-Sahara Africa—and it is declining by 20 years or more.[29]

The AIDS epidemic is not limited to Africa, however. Two countries in the Caribbean—Haiti and the Bahamas—are the worst hit outside the African continent, according to a United Nations report. The infection rates are five percent in Haiti and more than four percent in the Bahamas. AIDS has made inroads in Asia, too. According to a *New York Times* report (28 June 2000), the total number of people in India living with HIV was the second highest in the world behind South Africa. Although the statistic is difficult to verify, a shocking announcement from Chinese Minister of Health, Zhang Wenkang, at the U.N. summit on AIDS held in June 2001 in New York, to the effect that 600,000 people in China either had AIDS or were infected with HIV.[30]

Closer to home, reports showed a small but sharp rise in new HIV infections in San Francisco for 1997–1999. The *New York Times,* in a report on 1 July 2000, estimated that, despite aggressive prevention campaigns mounted in 1982, the number of new HIV infections in San Francisco had nearly doubled since 1996. The discovery gave no comfort to those who had hoped that the epidemic would be brought under control by the turn of the century.

Poverty is one more threat to human security. While an international conference on AIDS was being held in his country, President Thabo Mbeki of South Africa was quoted by the *New York Times,* 11 July 2000, as saying that "extreme poverty," rather than AIDS, was the "bigger killer" in South Africa. President Mbeki was supported by no less prestigious an environmentalist than Bjorn Lomborg, director of the Environmental Assessment Institute in Denmark, who believed that the world should "end global poverty before global warming."[31]

In closing this discussion, I wish to note the at-times close linkage among the three components of comprehensive security. The recent SARS attack on the Asian region is a ready example for this linkage. Although there is yet no consensus as to SARS' exact origin, the syndrome apparently resulted from less-than-sanitary conditions (hence, an environmental problem). Its victims included the hundreds of people stricken by the nontraditional virus, including those who perished (hence, an invasion of human security). The economy (an inroad of economic security) was another victim as the epidemic slowed production and trade; snarled business transactions; grounded flights; put travel and tourism at a halt; and created costs of premature deaths of income earners, lost work days of sick employees, higher hospitalization and treatment, and so on. Although a preliminary estimate of resulting costs was $11 billion, the final tally could be well over $50 billion.[32]

In sum, comprehensive security is going to gain increasing importance in the twenty-first century. The three forms of security under this generic rubric will compete with the traditional version of security (or national defense) for the attention of the security managers. After September 11, the traditional idea of national security has an antiterrorist offshoot, which has both an international orientation (as the target enemies are the faceless Al Qaeda legions and their affiliates scattered abroad) and a domestic defense line ("homeland security").

As such, the new antiterrorist brand of national security shares a commonality with comprehensive security in at least two senses: First, in both cases, the borders of a country are becoming less relevant as a shield against external threats to security. Second, in the antiterrorist security perspective, no less than in comprehensive security, individuals are more apt to be the first-line direct victims of an exogenous attack on one's country.

COMPREHENSIVE SECURITY
IN PACIFIC ASIA

In this section, we will examine the challenge to Pacific Asia in all three areas of comprehensive security as defined above. Although most of the problems are not limited to the Asian region alone, and some may be universal, we will note how the region reacts to these threats and if some lessons learned here may throw light on other regions.

ASIAN ECONOMIC SECURITY, FINANCIAL CRISIS
OF 1997–1999, AND THE FUTURE

Pacific Asia as a region enjoyed relative obscurity until the late 1980s, when its rapid economic growth—soaring in the six to nine percent range over the preceding two decades without slackening—first caught the fancy, even envy, of the wider world. According to a study of the World Bank, the region's eight "high-performance" economies[33] during 1960–1990 grew more than twice as fast as the rest of East Asia, roughly three times as fast as Latin America and South Asia, and twenty-five times faster than sub-Sahara Africa. These eight economies also significantly outperformed industrial economies and the oil-rich Middle East-North African region.[34]

At the rate of seven percent annual growth, which is double the normal growth rate of the older industrial economies (including the United States), an economy will double itself in one decade. Pacific Asia's phenomenal growth record, spreading from the original eight high-performance economies to other nations, prompted a wide range of respectable analysts to pronounce the twenty-first century to be the "Pacific Century."[35]

Rosy prognoses like these ought to be reassuring to the region's sense of economic security, although, reminiscent of the geopolitical power game, it might even inspire fears among many in other regions, typical of a "security dilemma"[36] although we have no proof of the existence of an economic security dilemma as such. But when the Asian financial crisis broke out on 2 July 1997, sending all the region's once-robust economies (except perhaps China, whose growth rates remained in the seven percent range throughout) into nosedives, none of the countries had illusions about any surety of economic security in this age of globalization.

In a matter of weeks, these once-robust economies and their strong currencies witnessed a meltdown. The severity of this meltdown can be appreciated only in comparison. During the Great Depression of 1929–1932, the asset value of Standard and Poor's 500 fell by 87 percent. During the Asian financial crisis, the asset value crash ranged from 75 to 85 percent in South Korea, Indonesia, Malaysia, and Thailand.[37]

Almost immediately after 2 July 1997, a swarm of sarcastic laments and gloating denunciations greeted the temporary misfortune besetting the Asian tigers. The former optimists and "apologists" for the Asian economic miracle were shut up. Instead, all that could be heard was the "I told you so" refrain from Western detractors, who had apparently had bottled-up contempt for the Asian tigers all along. Among the Western media and commentators was a chorus of voices of despair, even ridicule, but not a single word of sympathy, let alone a coolheaded plea for suspending final judgment until more was known about what had happened. Christopher Patten, the last British governor of Hong Kong before its return to China in 1997, could hardly wait to gloat with a petulant and, in a way, self-serving book celebrating "that all the tigers are skinned and stuffed" and heading for the museum.[38]

Instead of consolation, the Asian countries received ready-made condolences. Condemnation superseded commiseration and compassion, contrary to the expectations of basic human decency on such occasions of other people's sorrows. Like firefighters, the International Monetary Fund (IMF) was called on to help in its function as the lender of last resort. But, unlike firefighters, IMF was in no hurry to fight the fire on the scene. Instead, IMF took the time to point accusing fingers at the architecture of and furniture arrangement in the house.[39]

Despite IMF's initial gloomy forecasts that recovery would take years, if not decades, reports by early 1999 showed encouraging signs of rebound, even among the five worst-hit economies: Thailand, Indonesia, Korea, Malaysia, and the Philippines, although the first two were behind the rest on the way to recovery. In a review for the second half of 1999, the Asian Development Bank confirmed these reports.[40] Additionally, after a two-year, country-by-country study on the causes of the financial crisis and the patterns of recovery, a team of 15 economists hailing from 10 Asian countries and one economist from the United States also gave its concurring view that "[s]ince the summer of 1999, all the countries in the region have tended to gradually recover."[41]

The timing of recovery as such is not of itself important. What is important is the implicit but potent message that the recovery carries, or, in other words, the lessons we can learn from the reasons for the early onset of the reversal, which falsified the forecasts of IMF and many other Western analysts trained in laissez-faire economics. Although many lessons can be learned,[42] I shall focus on only a few that will not only explain the relative smooth turnaround but, more importantly, shed light on the future of economic security for the region, which is the real concern for this discussion.

First, from the experience of the financial crisis, we can safely conclude that a combination of three perverse factors had done the region in: (1) heavy foreign debt burden, (2) attacks by international currency speculators, and (3) loss of control by governments as a result of either laxity of laws and discipline or premature liberalization without due safeguard. Parenthetically, the Japanese case was slightly different, but even Japan had its ample share of loss of governmental control, as we will see below. Thailand, with a short-term, private-sector, foreign debt burden equivalent to 50 percent of its GDP, was the first to fall.[43] Devaluation of the Thai baht on 2 July 1997 sent rippling effects through Pacific Asia, affecting all its members, especially Korea, which was similarly ridden with huge short-term foreign debts. The rest was a story of chain reactions, known as "contagion" in technical parlance.[44]

In the search for an answer to the causes of their own weakness, especially their financial vulnerability, despite their robust growth, the region's governments were forced to face the reality that, although they all had strong manufacturing sectors, which had accounted for their growth, the countries' financial sectors were weak. The result of weak financial sectors was a general "inadequacy of financial regulation"[45] across the region. This weakness explains why the Asian governments hit by the financial crisis were ill-equipped to forestall the problems named as factors (1) through (3) above. The logical deduction from this flaw pointed to the C word (control) as a critical, relevant remedy.

Hence, these governments resorted to capital control in response to the economic challenge.[46] Malaysia, which had been among the most open economies on the capital account, went furthest in reintroducing capital controls. Beginning in August 1998, the exchange controls removed the Malay ringgit from international currency trading. The new system, patterned after China's preexisting model, made the ringgit convertible on the current account as before, but not on the capital account, thus preventing buying of foreign exchange for speculative purposes. Holders of offshore ringgit accounts had, in one month's time—September 1 to October 1—to repatriate their ringgits, after which repatriation would be illegal. Thus, contrary to fears of capital flight, imposition of exchange controls as such yielded a short-term, debt-free capital inflow.[47]

In similar fashion, governments elsewhere in the region (Hong Kong and Taiwan, for example) also intervened to protect stability in (read: maintain control over) the local stock and foreign-exchange markets and to fend off attacks by international speculators. In South Korea, where some capital account restrictions had been in place on the convertibility of the won, the government became more interventionist. In the financial sector, it moved fast to buy up bad loans from the banks and forced small banks to merge with larger ones.[48] The government adopted tighter monetary and fiscal policies and accepted slower growth to keep inflation below five percent and the current account deficit below one percent of GDP.[49] As elsewhere, these measures were taken to enhance governmental controls and not the structural reforms that Western critics had demanded.[50]

Thailand was the only exception in the region in that its government did not institute similar capital controls because after having used nearly all of its foreign reserves in its futile 1997 defense of the baht, the country had no reserves left to defend. It was entirely dependent on the IMF standby facility.[51]

These financial controls went against the teachings of laissez-faire economics and, equally, the counsels of globalization advocates. Undeniably, however, the controls proved instrumental in reversing the tides and re-steering the Asian economies to a path of steady recovery. The controls worked, precisely because they fulfilled a dual need of most nations in the region by (1) protecting against excessive inflows of foreign capital, especially short-term loans (i.e., the casino effects of hot money in and out) and, more importantly, (2) making the fairly open economies "less vulnerable to the whims and stampedes of portfolio and hedge fund managers" so as to reestablish stable growth following the whirlwind financial crisis.[52] I should add from the Asian experience that, in addition to capital control, the government in each case must have the ability to maintain price stability and high savings despite hardship. Currency control, in other words, worked only because it had the attendant support of sound economic fundamentals. Hence, currency control may not work in another region without similar supportive conditions.[53]

The second lesson we can learn from the Asian experience, building on the first lesson just noted, is that exogenous factors unquestionably accounted for more of the genesis of the Asian financial crisis than did domestic causes, such as nepotism and structural infirmities, at which many external critics had waggled giant fingers. We have already seen that the institution (or tightening up) of financial controls, rather than more un-safeguarded liberalization or deregulation, served the region's economies well in their recovery. Although Japan was a special case, it was different only because it did not have a full share of the first two of the three ills bedeviling the other Asian nations, marked (1) and (2) above. To wit, Japan did not have the same extent of the "heavy foreign debt problem" (although it had a different sort of problem brought on by foreign borrowings, as we will see), nor the same problem of "attacks by international speculators." Japan nevertheless shared part of the problem named as (3) above, to wit: "loss of control by governments, as a result of either laxity of laws and discipline or premature liberalization without due safeguard."

Concededly, the government-zaikai nepotism problem is notorious. It underscored Japan's one-and-a-half-decade-long economic downturn that predated the Asian crisis (as it began as early as 1989) and has continued long after other countries have resurged from the crisis of 1997–1999. Pessimism prevailing in almost all discussions of Japan's prospects of recovery is reflected in book titles such as *Can Japan Compete?* and *The Emptiness of Japanese Affluence.*[54]

But, as has been shown by the record, even overborrowing and corrupt banking systems were linked to external factors that compounded their deleterious effects, in the Japanese, as in other Asian, cases. First, overborrowing from foreign capital sources, usually in the form of loans denominated in the U.S. dollar, creating a crushing debt burden (more especially in the cases of Thailand and Korea), was because of the casino effect (hot money in and out) that came with globalization. The Japanese government's fault was that its control over borrowing by public and private end users was inadequate and hence, a monetary policy mismanagement. Second, although poorly regulated sectors may be a true flaw in some cases, domestic banking reform alone may not solve the whole problem. Take the Japanese banking system for example. The Japanese banks' trouble can be traced back to Tokyo's unguarded deregulation in the 1980s, when they were under pressure from the G-7 and the 1985 Plaza Accord. Despite its supposed virtues, deregulation opened the Japanese capital market to global capital inflows—and removed the Japanese banks' monitoring function on corporate performance of the borrowing enterprises, to boot. It also greatly enhanced equity financing by the so-called "nonbanks" (e.g., manufacturing firms) for Japan's medium and small enterprises that could not borrow from the foreign capital markets. In the process, this change robbed the Japanese banks of their core loan market, shrinking it to a third of its previous level by the end of the 1980s. As Sunday Owuala points out, the ensuing competition forced the banks to "engage in speculative lending in property and stocks for survival." The collapse of both property and stock prices at the beginning of the 1990s, he adds, "left on the trail a huge volume of non-performing assets in many banks."[55] If indeed this was the case, Japan would need to moderate its unguarded banking deregulation as well as tighten control over borrowing from the international financial market. Both actions would go against the counsels usually heard from Western economists about Japan's "nepotic" banking system!

The future of the Pacific Asian region's economic security, therefore, depends on two closely related conditions. First, whether the measures that the Asian governments instituted in response to the crisis—that is, measures that have been responsible for bailing them out and bringing about their relatively smooth and, in some cases, even speedy recoveries—will remain in place, immunizing them from similar attacks in the future. Second, of the three factors we identified above as being responsible for the onset of the crisis, only the first (overborrowing from the global monetary market)[56] and the last (inadequate financial regulation) are within the grasp of governments. In fact, the capital control mechanisms instituted by the Asian governments, as noted before, should insulate them against the said problems, provided that the existing sound economic fundamentals continue in place. Attacks by international currency speculators—or what Paul Krugman calls "masters of the universe: hedge funds and other villains"[57]—however, cannot be coped with by any government acting alone. External speculators, such as the ones whose manipulations brought on the Asian financial crisis, operate in the dark and get away with predatory "killings" because no international rules and mechanisms (regimes) exist to restrain them.[58]

The recent Asian experience provides a justification for the creation of international regimes for the control and restraint of international currency speculation. Although the Pacific Asian region, in the aftermath of the crisis, has established a modest early warning system,[59] the task requires further collective efforts, eventually at the global level.[60] While these efforts are yet to be forthcoming, the heightened sense of Asian regionalism, as shown in the expansion of ASEAN to ten members and the hatching of an ASEAN-China free trade area,[61] is a healthy development for the future of the region's economic security.

HUMAN SECURITY IN PACIFIC ASIA

Unlike certain other parts of the world, the Pacific Asian region has only remote memories of Kosovo-type genocidal conflicts. No similar attacks on human security of the kind found in Bosnia, Burundi, and Rwanda (besides Kosovo), were heard of, at least in the final two decades of the twentieth century. It remains sadly true, however, that Cambodia (briefly known as Kampuchia) under the Pol Pot regime, 1975–1979, was the first state after the end of World War II to commit war crimes against its own population. In four years' time, Pol Pot's Khmer Rouge regime was credited with having slaughtered three million people, roughly one-third of its population, approaching half of the six million victims of the Holocaust over 12 years (1933–1945). Although the Nazis killed ethnic Jews in Germany, Pol Pot killed his own kin—his fellow Cambodians. The dire magnitude of the Cambodian genocidal crimes remains unparalleled in peacetime anywhere in the world. A greater tragedy is that perhaps because these heinous crimes against humanity were committed in Asia, they have never received the same amount of worldwide attention as did the ethnic cleansings in Bosnia and Kosovo, not to mention the Holocaust in Nazi Germany. Like the World War II crimes and atrocities against humanity committed by the Japanese army in Asia,[62] these heinous crimes in Pol Pot's Cambodia have received far less condemnation in the West.

In developing countries, poverty is a basic source of human insecurity.[63] Fortunately, poverty is not a widespread problem in the Pacific Asian region. The region nevertheless has a few problems of its own, notably income inequality, aging, racial conflicts, cross-boundary drug trafficking, and the plight of women's rights, which we will discuss separately below.

Income inequities. Although no in-depth comparative studies of income inequality across the Pacific Asia is known to me, the problem of income inequity seems to me more pronounced in the wealthier countries. For example, in Singapore, according to a government survey released in May 2000, monthly household income for the bottom 10 percent of the population fell to S$133 (U.S.$76.87) in 1999 from S$258 (U.S.$149.13) the preceding year. At the same time, the richest 20 percent of households made 18 times what was earned by the poorest 20 percent of households—up from 15 times in 1998.[64] Hong Kong is not much better. Although little or no information is readily available about the six years since the territory's return to Chinese sovereignty in 1997, a period marred first by the Asian financial crisis and, more recently, by the SARS attack, available data for the colonial period showed a gloomy picture almost as bad as that of Singapore. During 1976–1991, the top 10 percent of the population in Hong Kong earned eight times as much as the bottom 10 percent. The gap was widening instead of narrowing. Over the eleven-year period of 1986–1996, the top 20 percent of wage earners sported a hefty 60 percent increase in income. The bottom 20 percent of all wage earners, however, had only a 20 percent pay rise.[65]

Neoclassical economic historians argue that income inequality often increases in the early stages of industrialization but that structural changes resulting from the transition will eventually lead to a more equitable distribution of income. The question is how long the transition is going to be before the assumed self-correcting change will balance out the gross inequities. During the indefinite transition, the continuing, and often widening, income gulfs pose a dire problem for human security.

The aging problem. Aging is a universal problem in Pacific Asia. In China, for example, a People's University study shows that by the mid-21st century, one-fifth of the Chinese population will be at least 60 years old, while 80 million (seven times the number in the year 2000) Chinese will be octogenarians (Qiaobao [*The China Press,* New York], 20 October 2000, p. 5). The dubious honor of having the most serious aging problem falls on Japan, however. Aggregate data show that Japan is aging faster than any other nation in the world. With 17 percent of the Japanese population aged 65 or over, including 7 percent in the 75 or above group, it has the highest percentage of the elderly in its population. (By comparison, 10 percent of China's 1.2 billion people are over the age of 60.) Before 2010, one in every five Japanese will be a senior citizen. In 2050, the number will increase to one in three.[66] According to a *New York Times* report (23 July 2003), by the mid-21st century, Japan will have 30 percent fewer people and one million 100-year-olds. By then, 800,000 more people will die each year than are born. By century's end, the United Nations estimates, the present population of 120 million will be cut in half. This graying phenomenon creates not only a caring problem for the elderly but also an increasing burden for the country's old-age welfare programs. It also raises a serious labor shortage that Japan has to grapple with, forcing the country to confront the once-taboo option of importing labor from abroad. Despite Japan's xenophobic immigration policy, more and more business executives are calling on the government to open the country to foreign workers. In a shocking report released in 2000, the United Nations projected that Japan would need to import 609,000 immigrants a year to maintain its 1995 working-age population level of 87.2 million through 2050. If Japan follows this advice, the report says, 30 percent of the country's population would be immigrants or their descendents by the mid-twenty-first century.[67]

Racial Conflicts. As a source of human insecurity, racial conflicts have a long history in Southeast Asia, an area of a multiracial community, where the major division in many countries is between the Malays and the Chinese. Most ex-colonial countries in the area bear a continuing grudge against their colonial heritage for the introduction of Chinese into the Malay world. In the nineteenth century, Chinese were imported by colonial rulers for coolie labor in their Malay-populated colonies. In a strange twist of history, descendants of these earlier Chinese coolies now dominate the economy in many of the ex-colonial Southeast Asian countries.[68] Bi-communal conflicts rocked the first years of postcolonial Singapore. The underlying animosity between the Chinese and the Malays was a cause for Singapore's short-lived federation with Malaya to form the new Malaysia during 1963–1965.[69] In the neighboring Malaysia, riots and clashes between the Malay majority and the Chinese minority during 1969–1971 even triggered a brief period of martial law.[70] The jitters created by these conflicts have intimidated the Singaporean Chinese ever since, although Singaporean Chinese make up 76.4 percent of the local population to the Malays' 14.9 percent. The timid Chinese in Singapore are keenly aware that they are besieged by a sea of Malays in neighboring countries, from Malaysia and Indonesia to the Philippines.

The most gruesome of recurrent racial attacks on the Chinese minority was in Indonesia. An example was the riots of May 13–15, 1998, which broke out following a shoot-out by security forces that killed four students during an antigovernment demonstration at Trsakti University in Jakarta. The horrifying atrocities committed by the rioters against the ethnic Chinese were not fully known until weeks later after the Joint Fact-Finding Team (TGPF) concluded its investigation. The TGPF report showed a casualty list for the ethnic Chinese that included many among the 1,198 persons murdered (including 27 shot) and 31 missing; 40 shopping centers burned; 4,083 shops burned; 1,026 houses gutted; and 168 girls and women raped.[71]

Mounting evidence suggests that the riots, originally believed to be spontaneous outbursts, were masterminded to deliberately target the Chinese, with complicity by elements of the Indonesian security forces. Reports alleged that ethnic Chinese women raped in the riots were victims of organized sexual attacks. Similarly, the killing and sacking of the Chinese and their properties were the result of racially motivated assaults. The Chinese, who made up a bare 4 percent of the Indonesian population, were blamed for "not repaying the community," despite their wealth.[72]

If their numerical minority combined with their success in the local economy was indeed the ultimate source of grief for the ethnic Chinese in Indonesia, the same symbiosis is repeated elsewhere, in Malaysia, Thailand, the Philippines, and so on. However, in Indonesia, the trouble for the Chinese minority was further complicated by the dubious role of the military, which was implicated in the 1998 riots, and, more specifically, in the way the riots turned on their allegedly targeted victims in Jakarta, as later in East Timor and Aceh.[73] Admittedly, Indonesia is a country simultaneously plagued by sectarian violence, separatist movements, and political disarray complicated by a too-autonomous military, so the racial problem confronting the Chinese there may be peculiarly acute. Only in Malaysia, however, among all Malay-dominated countries in the region, was the Chinese minority ever able to secure an agreement on "power sharing" with the local ethnic majority.[74] Barring future similar developments elsewhere, racial conflicts similar to those that erupted in Indonesia in 1998 can be expected to recur, though not necessarily to the same degree of gruesome violence and destruction. I wish to point out, nonetheless, that any racial conflict, even if the ethnic Chinese or any other minority should be the alleged target victim, will claim a gratuitous additional toll on other groups, including members of the ethnic majority that happen to be in harm's way. In this sense, racial conflicts as such are a real, though occasional, harrying challenge to human security in Pacific Asian countries with large "bio-communal" makeups in their populations.

Drug Trafficking. Illicit drug trafficking is another source of human insecurity haunting the Asian region. The production and consumption of narcotic substances have a long history in East Asia, but several disturbing new developments have forced narcotics trafficking onto the regional security agenda for the first time.[75] First, once primarily a producer of heroin shipped to other parts of the world, East Asia has itself become a major heroin consumer and an emerging market for a new class of designer drugs such as "ice" and "ecstasy." Drug dependency in countries with no record of drug addiction in recent decades (e.g., China and Vietnam) is rising at an alarming rate. Secondly, narcotics trafficking is a new multibillion-dollar business in East Asia; it was probably the only enterprise not affected by the recent economic crisis gripping the region. Drug money is distorting the region's economies and exacerbating corruption and political instability. At a Steering Committee meeting held in Canberra, Australia, on 10 December 1996, the Council for Security Cooperation in the Asia Pacific (CSCAP) decided to establish a study group on transnational crime, including drug trafficking.[76] This development is a clear indication that the region's vigilance has been aroused by the rise of the drug problem as a threat to human security.

Women's Rights. Contrary to the expectations of detractors of Confucian values, the worst case of women's rights is in Japan, whose culture is predominantly Shinto-influenced and only peripherally touched by the Confucian culture. In comparison with other countries in the region, Japan's influence from Confucianism is probably the lowest, yet Japan's record of women's rights is indisputably one of the worst in the world. In Japan, the privileges of manhood are still deeply entrenched, more so than elsewhere. In the job market, men are hired with the general assumption that they will build careers with their companies; women are typically separated into one of two categories—*ippan shoku* (miscellaneous workers) and *sogo shoku* (a career track). The miscellaneous female workers, who are still legion in every Japanese ministry and large company and are known as "office ladies," or O.L.s, will rarely rise above their lowly status and enter career tracks, which are still largely reserved for males. Among female workers, who make up 41 percent of the Japanese population, only a sparing 8.9 percent are classified as managerial workers, compared to 46.6 percent and 46 percent, respectively, in the United States.[77] Despite the passage of a landmark antidiscrimination law in 1985 and its reinforcement in 1999 with amendments that include sanctions against sexual harassment, many Japanese companies still maintain the separate-track personnel management system.[78] Despite the nation's steep population decline and acute labor shortage, the same practice dies hard. Keeping women sidelined like this is not just a deprivation of their human security; it has economic costs that have been felt acutely only during the country's 13 years of economic stagnation. A study presented to the Labor Ministry estimates that the lack of women's full economic participation may be shaving 0.6 percent off Japan's annual growth. In 2003 the World Economic Forum ranked Japan number 69 of 75 total member nations on empowering women. As Mariko Bando, an aide to Prime Minister Koizumi, remarked to reporters, "Japan is still a developing country in terms of gender equality."[79]

Similar problems confront women's rights elsewhere in Pacific Asia, but they may not necessarily all result from indigenous culture. In some cases, the problems may be traced to an unfinished chapter in colonial legacy. One of the two last places to exit from Western colonial rule in the region is Hong Kong, which may offer an example. In this former British colony, sexual discrimination against women continued to exist even after the New Territories ordinance that had deprived women of land inheritance rights was amended in 1994 under the departing colonial government. According to an authority on the subject, the practices of discrimination against women resulting from the lack of equal opportunity protection by law—that is, practices that have been abolished in other Chinese societies—were "frozen in time by colonial ordinances" in Hong Kong.[80] I might mention the long-standing colonial policy of tolerating concubinage as one of the things "frozen" in time. Additionally, even after the enactment of the Bill of Rights under the British post-1989 campaign to democratize on the verge of their 1997 departure, 50 existing (colonial period) laws were inconsistent with the International Covenant for Civil and Political Rights, to which Hong Kong became a party as a British colony. Likewise, many colonial-age laws ran afoul of the Convention on the Elimination of All Forms of Discrimination Against

Women (CDAW), which became applicable to Hong Kong after 1976. Whatever was not rectified under the outgoing British rulers devolved upon the post-handover government of the Hong Kong Special Administrative Region (SAR) after 1 July 1997.[81]

Regardless of their origins, native culture, or vestiges of colonial neglect, injustices against women's rights are a formidable challenge to a very real part of human security in Pacific Asia.

ENVIRONMENTAL SECURITY IN PACIFIC ASIA

Strictly speaking, Pacific Asia is much broader in the geographical expanse it covers than East and Southeast Asia. Geographically, the Pacific region is vast; the Pacific is the world's largest ocean, studded by thousands of islands grouped into about 30 political territories. The Pacific islands are usually associated with high levels of "biophysical vulnerability," or the potential for loss from natural hazards, environmental variability, and change. One of the most widely popularized environmental threats to the region is contamination from nuclear waste dumping and weapons testing. The testing of thermonuclear weapons in the region (by the United States) began in 1946.[82]

During the Cold War and well into the postcolonial period, the Pacific region remained of strategic military significance to the United States. It is of continuing strategic importance in terms of access to international transport lines, seabed resources, fisheries, and natural resources. Conflicts over resources and the environment may intensify because of expanding interests from Asian governments and private companies offshore.[83]

For our discussion here, four issue areas warrant special attention on the environmental security of the Pacific Asian region at large. They are (a) threats of sea-level rises, caused by global warming, to the archipelagic and island states and the littoral states with long coastlines; (b) the future of shared resources; (c) air pollution and recurrent forest fires; and (d) growing terrorism and maritime piracy.

First, except for landlocked Laos, the countries in East and Southeast Asia are surrounded by the ocean; Indonesia and the Philippines are archipelagic states.[84] Japan is made up of four major islands and other lesser islands. Singapore is a tiny island city-state. China, Malaysia, Vietnam, and, to a lesser extent, Cambodia and Thailand, have long coastlines. On a global scale, our ecosystem's climate temperature is steadily rising because of increased concentrations of carbon dioxide and other gases trapped in the atmosphere. The threatened rise in sea levels as a result of global warming, therefore, poses hazards for all of Pacific Asia. As noted above, if the rates of increase in trapped gases continue, the sea level is expected to rise by up to one meter by 2100.[85] It is mind-boggling to imagine the effects of such a rise in sea levels on residents and businesses near the shorelines in these archipelagic and littoral states, and in such other places as Japan, Singapore, and Hong Kong, resulting from the consequential flooding and intrusion of salt water into estuaries and groundwater, not to mention the inundation of beaches and waterfront properties. Infectious diseases, from the dengue epidemic to bird flu (which haunted the Hong Kong area in 1999), the latter causing one million chickens to be slaughtered, were additional grave reminders of the effects of environmental degradation and that the environment could be a real threat to the region's security. As if to warn that such effects know of no territorial or temporal limit, the return of the nipah virus in 1999 killed more than 100 people and led to the slaughter of more than one million pigs both in peninsular Malaysia and, of much more worry, in the Borneo state of Sarawak,[86] about 400 miles across the South China Sea from Malaysia. The most recent epidemic to hit the Pacific Asian region was the SARS virus, which broke out in the spring of 2003, disrupting international travel and inflicting untold damages on the region's economy, as already noted.

Second, disputes over the control of shared resources (such as shared water of international rivers) may lead to conflicts, and renewable resources (fish stocks, for example) may be depleted because of conflict. In the larger Pacific Asian region, at least three areas of shared resources exist, one of which is the South China Sea, with its rich fishing grounds and oil and gas deposits. The other two are the international Mekong River and the sea lanes connecting Northeast Asia, through the Taiwan Strait, the South China Sea, and various "choke points" in Southeast Asia, to the Indian Ocean and points beyond.[87] The salience of the sea lanes is tied to the region's 60 percent dependence on Middle Eastern oil. A mitigating circumstance, though, is China's deliberate reliance on oil and gas from Central Asia and its vast resources in Xingjiang under development. Consistent with the same policy, during President Hu Jingtao's visit to Moscow in May 2003, China and Russia signed an agreement under which the Russians will transport oil from Western Siberia to China's Daqing Oilfield, to the order of 5.13 billion barrels annually from 2005 through 2030.[88]

The South China Sea is the best-known hotbed of disputes of the three areas, ostensibly because two internationally contested outlying island groups are located in its waters. The Paracels are claimed by Vietnam and China, which have fought two wars over the islands, in 1974 and again in 1988. To the Spratlys, the other outlying island group, seven parties, including China, Vietnam, Malaysia, Indonesia, Brunei, Taiwan, and the Philippines, have laid overlapping claims.[89] Although much of the existing literature on disputes in the South China Sea approaches the disputes from a geostrategic point of view, I would, in the present context, call attention to the contested shared resources as a crucial factor behind the disputes. For instance, an occasion for a Sino-Vietnamese verbal skirmish was the announced signing by China of an agreement with Creston Energy Co., a Denver-based U.S. company, for oil exploration in the South China Sea (*New York Times,* 18 June 1992). Immediately, the Vietnamese Foreign Ministry issued a statement denouncing the move as contravening Vietnamese sovereignty, because Vietnam also claims the same area covered by the Chinese agreement.[90]

Another instance of dispute was that arising from Malaysia's arrest of four Taiwanese fishing vessels for illegal fishing in Malaysia's waters in August 1988.[91] In these and other cases, if disputes lead to armed conflicts, they would likely inflict irreparable damages to the contested shared resources at stake, hence leading to a breach of the region's environmental security.

The long, meandering stretch of land traversed by the Mekong River is an area where potential disputes may lead to similar consequences. The Mekong runs a course of 2,600 miles, from southern China through Myanmar (Burma), Laos, Thailand, and Cambodia to Vietnam, where it exits into the South China Sea. Conflict potential is especially high where the river forms the border between Myanmar and western Laos, and later between

Laos and Thailand. From the ecopolitical point of view, that belt is the site of potential future conflicts, for it is home to 230 million people, many living in poverty. Already, the ASEAN has a developmental project known as the Greater Mekong Sub-region (GMS) program with more than 100 "priority projects," including the construction of highway and railway links and dozens of hydroelectric dams on the Mekong and its tributaries, at a projected cost of up to $1 billion (*The Economist,* 7 September 1996, pp. 31–32).

For China, the Mekong offers a link with Southeast Asia and a chance to develop Yunan, one of its poorest provinces. But for the poorer countries, GMS offers a dream of prosperity, although the poorest, Laos, is rightfully the most cautious, ever fearful that its natural wealth will be carved up by overbearing neighbors. The potential for both mutual benefit and suspicion is seen most clearly in the ASEAN plans for the river. Although the river affords much hope for hydroelectric power generation, those countries with the biggest demand for electricity are not necessarily the ones with the biggest hydroelectric potential. For instance, Thailand has the greatest need for electricity but the least hydroelectric potential (see chart in *The Economist,* 7 September, 1996, 12). Many environmentalists, already horrified, warn of problems ranging from the intrusion of salt water into the delta to the loss of fish and rare mammals. China, thus far, is damming the main stream of the Mekong. The anxiety of the downstream countries is clearly understandable. If disputes over sharing water resources and control of water pollution along the Mekong River, as elsewhere, cannot be peacefully worked out by its riparian states, conflict is a most likely staple in the relations among the nations involved.

A possible solution to these and other similar disputes involving shared resources and environmental control is to follow a precedent set by China and Vietnam in 1993. In October of that year, the two countries reached an agreement whereby they pledged to suspend, without prejudice, their respective claims to the Paracel Islands in the interest of joint peaceful exploration of its resources (*China Daily,* 21 October 1993).[92] Conceivably, the same formula could be used in the resolution of disputes over the Spratlys and other sites, such as the oil-rich Tiaoyutai/Senkaku island, a long-standing source of friction between Japan and China.

Third, although air pollution such as that caused by industrial waste, tailpipe emissions, and the like is a universal problem, the Asian region has had more than its share of the problem. In Hong Kong, one of Asia's richest cities, for example, wealth has begotten waste, and lots of it—on an average day, about 16,000 tons of garbage go to landfills. Another 15 million tons of sewage, enough to fill 1,000 Olympic-size swimming pools, spill into Victoria Harbor daily. Diesel-powered taxis and trucks rumble through the city's streets, leaving pedestrians cupping hands over mouths, trying not to inhale the air. Polluted air is blamed for 2,000 premature deaths a year. "Some in Hong Kong Are Fed Up With Smog," ran a headline in the *Asian Wall Street Journal Weekly* (July 3–9, 2000, p. 1).

What is true of Hong Kong is also true of many other cities in the region. Yet, as if this were not enough, recurrent forest fires in Indonesia present another nuisance for the environment far beyond Indonesia's borders. For instance, a forest and land fire started in mid-1997 burned and smoldered for more than one year. It finally burned out in East Kalimantan in May 1998, but not before it had scorched at least 500,000 hectares (1.4 billion acres) of land. For the entire year, the haze not only blanketed vast areas of East Kalimantan but also reached far-off points in Malaysia, Singapore, the Philippines, and other parts of Southeast Asia.[93]

Details of these fires need not concern us except that Indonesia's apparent inability to prevent and control the wildfires is a source of worry for its neighbors. The same causes and neglect were said to be responsible for earlier recurrent fires in the country in 1986, 1991, and 1994. These wildfires have almost always been human-caused, such as those resulting from agricultural conversion burns (to prepare land for pulp wood and oil palm plantations), logging operations, and even arson.[94]

The recurrence rate of these wildfires seems to have only increased. In March 2000, about 1,200 fires were reported in the Indonesian provinces of Riau on Sumatra and Kalimantan on Borneo, with pollution readings over the 300 level on the Pollution Standard Index (PSI), a level considered hazardous to health. The pollution effects spilled into neighboring countries. In nearby Singapore, for example, the air quality worsened to the most polluted levels of the year on March 8, when its PSI stood at 65. Malaysian environmentalists expected their country to feel the effects of the haze if the fires continued.[95] Again, in July 2001 (the latest information available to me at the time of writing), wildfires on the Indonesian Islands of Sumatra and Kalimantan (Borneo) created a dense smoky haze blanketing a large swath of Southeast Asia. Nonetheless, Indonesia's inability to prevent slash-and-burn agriculture by both large estate and small private farms that caused the wildfires, and its failure to formulate a plan of action to fight the fires, has exacerbated what has become an almost annual event.[96]

Estimates of the damage of these fires to the global environment are both hard to come by and time-consuming. In late 2002, the Environmental News Service (ENS) carried a report on the final estimates, made by a team of British scientists, of the 1997 wildfires in Indonesia. According to these estimates by the team headed by Susan Page from the University of Leicester, United Kingdom, the fires that scorched parts of Indonesia in 1997 "spewed as much carbon into the atmosphere as the entire planet's biosphere removes from it in a year." The fires released as much as 2.6 billion metric tons of carbon—mostly in the form of the greenhouse gas carbon dioxide (CO_2)—into the atmosphere. The conclusion of the team's study was that the Indonesian fires were "a major contributor to the sharp increase in atmospheric CO_2 concentrations detected in 1998."[97] Thus, the Indonesian recurrent wildfires are not just a regional problem threatening only the environmental security of Southeast Asia, but a global warming problem.

Fourth, terrorism in the Pacific Asian region became a festering, albeit underreported, problem even before the September 11 sneak attacks on New York and Washington made the whole world edgy about terror. On 23 April 2000, armed men representing the Philippine separatist Abu Sayaf Group (ASG) raided the Malaysian diving resort of Sipadan and seized more than 21 tourists from Malaysia, Germany, South Africa, Lebanon, Finland, and the Philippines. Using these people as hostages, the terrorists entered into negotiations with the Philippine government. They made a variety of demands, including the creation of a separate state and the restoration of fishing rights for local fishermen. A few weeks later, the ASG began demanding a $1 million ransom for each hostage. They seized additional hostages, including foreign journalists covering the story. By August 2000, the group had reportedly taken in more than $5.5 million in ransom money.[98] The ASG is a threat to not only the Philippines but also to the larger region, as it was known to have links with extremist Islamic groups in the Middle East and South Asia.[99] One such link was with Osama bin Laden, who had reportedly funneled financial support and deployed trainers to the ASG, as well as to another local terrorist group, the Moro Islamic Liberation Front (MILF).

As recently as 6 August 2003, a sport utility vehicle packed with explosives blew up in the Indonesian capital of Jakarta, killing 15 people and wounding 150 in a Marriott Hotel, a large restaurant, and an office building. The police, three days later, identified the suicide bomber as Asmar Latin Sani, a new recruit of the militant Islamic group Jemaah Islamiyah, which is known to have close ties with Al Qaeda. Indonesian experts believed that the group's operatives planned and carried out the attack in Bali in October 2002, in which seven Americans were among the 202 killed (*New York Times,* 6 August 2003, p. 1; and 9 August 2003, p. 9).

The world's most virulent outbreak of chemical- and biological-weapons terrorism to date took place in East Asia. The Japanese cult Aum Shinrikyo, in March 1995, released sarin nerve gas in the Tokyo subway system, killing eleven people and injuring more than 5,000. As subsequent investigations revealed, the group had attempted other chemical-biological weapons attacks, including an unsuccessful attempt to kill thousands of Tokyo residents by releasing anthrax spores from a tall building (*New York Times,* 26 May 1998, p. 1).[100]

Maritime piracy, a problem related to terrorism, presents another hazard for the Pacific Asian region's security in more than just the environmental sense. One instance of maritime piracy happened to a Hong Kong-owned cargo ship, the Cheung Son. On 16 November 1998, while traveling from Shanghai to Malaysia, the ship lost contact with its owners as it passed through the Taiwan Strait. The ship was attacked by a gang of pirates who were able to board by posing as antismuggling police. Once aboard the ship, the pirates ordered the 23-member crew to lie on the floor, where they were bound, gagged, and blindfolded. After executing the crew by machine guns and other weapons, the pirates then methodically weighted the bodies and tossed them overboard. Many of the bodies later turned up in fishermen's nets. The attack on the Cheung Son was one of the most violent maritime attacks in Eastern Asia in recent years. Although Chinese authorities eventually caught most of the perpetrators, it is a fact of life that sophisticated syndicates view maritime piracy as simply another means of making fast, though illicit, profits.[101]

The greatest threat of maritime piracy is still in Southeast Asia, especially in waters around Indonesia and the Philippines, both archipelagic countries. According to one account, nearly two-thirds of the world's maritime piracy attacks in 1999 occurred in Asia, and about 113 (40 percent) of the 285 reported cases of piracy in the region took place in Indonesia's ports and territorial waters.[102]

Rising maritime piracy in the Asian region in recent times has largely correlated with its economic and political problems resulting from the 1997 financial crisis. In Indonesia, political instability associated with the conditions surrounding the ouster of General Suharto, and the economic malaise magnified by the Asian financial crisis, have been linked to rising pirate activity, perhaps because of reduced funding for law enforcement or naval patrols. Skyrocketing unemployment may have turned many people, conceivably even some legitimate sailors, to piracy. Another reason that maritime piracy is thriving in Southeast Asia is the lack of a coordinated regional approach to the problem. In areas where governments are known to have weak law enforcement and where states engage in competing territorial claims, the pirates find their most fertile operating grounds.[103] Mutual suspicion between governments remains the toughest obstacle to any collaborative antipiracy efforts on a regional level and spells a blessing for the pirates preying on ships that ply the region's waters.

SUMMARY AND COMMENTARY

SUMMARY

In our search for the meaning and ramifications of comprehensive security in Pacific Asia, we have looked at the economic, human, and environmental components of the question. In this closing section, I pause to sum up the main findings and then venture a commentary. The following is a summary of the findings.

First, economic security is distinctly the region's longest suit, not only because of its proven record of sustained, robust growth reaching "miraculous" proportions, but also because it has passed the trying test of the Asian financial crisis, mostly with flying colors.[104] Paul Stiglitz, who supervised the World Bank's earlier study, *The East Asian Miracle* (1993), led a reevaluative study of the Pacific Asian economies bruised by the crush of the crisis of 1997. The purpose of the study was to learn if any new insights could be gained from a "rethinking" of the miracle thesis advanced earlier. Fifteen eminent scholars, hailing from four countries (Japan, Malaysia, China, and the U.S.) and Hong Kong, took part in the project. The result was a monograph, *Rethinking the East Asian Miracle* (2001), which Stiglitz coedited with Shahid Yusuf. While most chapters are country-oriented, the final chapter, by Stiglitz, sums everything up at the regional level. For the question "Was there a miracle?" the inevitable conclusion, after careful "rethinking," is that the East Asian record of growth deserves the epithet "miracle," or any other synonymous superlative. As if to warn the remaining skeptics, Stiglitz adds that "there is another aspect of the miracle that has received too little attention but plays a role in the sequel: capitalism has always been plagued by fluctuations, including financial panics." The Asian miracle can be appreciated only through comparison. What is remarkable about East Asia, Stiglitz points out, is not that it so successfully passed the test of the 1997–1999 crisis but that it "had experienced so few crises over the preceding three decades." This, he emphasizes, is "a better record than any of the supposedly advanced and well-managed Organization of Economic Cooperation and Development (OECD) countries" (p. 510).

Despite the debilitating SARS epidemic that hit China from November 2002 through June 2003, a forecast by the *Wall Street Journal* (14 July 2003, p. 1) said that the Chinese economy would sustain an 8 percent GDP growth rate for the year. According to statistics released by the National Statistic Bureau in Beijing on 17 April 2003, China's GDP had already registered a whopping 9.9 percent growth during the first quarter of the year.[105]

Second, the Pacific Asian region's record on human security is spotty. Although the lack of the abject poverty problem that usually afflicts developing countries is positive, the region suffers from a number of problems of its own, as we have noted. Some of these, such as income inequities and the denial of women's rights, are found in other parts of the world but are more acute in the Asian region. Certain other problems may also appear elsewhere but are different in nature in the Asian region—for example, drug trafficking. If, in Latin America, drug pushers deal in cocaine, Asian drug dealers concentrate on heroin trafficking. Still other problems are either so much more severe or so different in Asia that they stand out in comparison with the rest of the world. Japan's aging problem is probably the most severe among all known cases anywhere. Without doubt, Japan's problem with women's rights is the most severe among industrialized countries. Whereas racial conflicts are known in many other places, the bi-communal (Malay-Chinese) conflicts in Southeast Asian countries are unique in terms of their frequency, intensity, and extent of violence involved. Other problems such as illegal migration and human smuggling, which we did not discuss earlier, are likewise very real threats to human security at both the micro (individual) and macro (society) levels in the region.[106] Most disheartening is the reported transborder trafficking of women and children, by the hundreds of thousands, annually in Southeast Asia.[107]

Third, on environmental security, Pacific Asia has more than its share of the hazards and inroads that one may find in other regions. Heading the list is the threat of sea-level rises caused by global warming, which is particularly worrisome, as the region abounds in island nations and archipelagic states as well as littoral countries with long coastlines. Other problems include those confronting shared resources, air pollution and wildfires, growing terrorism, and maritime piracy. Two of these (man-made Indonesian wildfires and maritime piracy) are endemic to the region.

The above summary opens the way to a commentary, as follows.

COMMENTARY AND LOOKING AHEAD

Given this "report card" on how the Asian region is faring in respect of the three component parts of comprehensive security, what is the "bottom line" as to whether and how the Pacific Asian region can do better in anticipation of the time ahead as compared with other regions? Of the three previously discussed findings, our safest bet is that the region's smallest worry is economic security. If anything, in light of the lessons from the recent financial crisis, the area states could invest more collaborative energies in mapping ways to ward off future attacks by international currency speculators. Unlike economic security, environmental security is the region's Achilles' heel, and the many environmental security problems defy single-nation solutions. The problems require multination collaboration at the regional level, at a minimum, which is especially true of transnational crimes such as terrorism and maritime piracy, which have become increasingly virulent since the financial crisis of 1997. If Pacific Asian countries are to cope with these threats effectively, they must cooperate in the most intimate ways possible. They need to share tactical intelligence, build mutual trust, and put aside political rivalries and suspicion to address the wider concerns. But this is easier said than done. As Paul Smith[108] points out, mutual suspicion thwarts any wish for a regional approach. One example was seen when Japan proposed deploying its coast guard in joint patrols to help fight piracy in the region; the suggestion received cool responses from neighboring countries, which still remember the atrocities committed during the Japanese aggression in the 1930s and 1940s and thus have reasons to fear Japan's military presence in the region. On this, as on other issues (such as Japan's bid for a permanent seat on the U.N. Security Council), the neighboring nations' suspicions and distrust will not subside before and unless Tokyo is ready to acknowledge its past aggression and atrocities and apologize to its Asian neighbors, an action that Japan's neighbors have demanded repeatedly, in vain.[109]

In conclusion, the ultimate challenge to Pacific Asia in the age of comprehensive security is for the region's nations, each of which is doing well in its own way on the economic security front, to learn to collaborate as a region to combat the threats to their environmental and human security. The prospect over the long run is, however, not as dim as it looks, for two reasons. The first is based on the region's experience in the recent crisis, in reaction to which member states collaborated, for instance, to establish an early warning system against future signs of another such dire threat to their economic security. It proves that, given time and a grave-enough threat, the region can rise to the occasion.

The second reason for optimism comes from a preliminary reading of the ongoing power realignments in the larger area of "Asia Pacific," which in our definition denotes the Pacific Asian region plus North America (the United States included). Already, a positive development has occurred across the Pacific all the way to the shores of America. Long before September 11, China and the United States had joined hands in the fight against drug trafficking in the Asian region. For a few years, their law enforcement agencies have cooperated occasionally to stop contraband drug shipments. The two countries signed an agreement on 19 June 2000 to increase cooperation in the fight against illegal drugs, especially heroin and methamphetamine (*New York Times*, 20 June 2000, p. 11). Concededly, beyond the immediate step of international cooperation in interdicting drug supplies, much more work needs to be done in the rehabilitation of the addicts, which requires joint action by national governments in the region. But the U.S.-Chinese bilateral collaboration is a good start, for the experience thus gained, and the cooperative habit formed, could pave the way for expanding the efforts in other pursuits such as eradicating human trafficking, maritime piracy, and so on. The collaboration could also entice other governments to join, thus expanding the currently bilateral efforts into a region-wide network for combating international crimes and terrorism. In the post-9/11 fight against terrorism, U.S. cooperation with China and Southeast Asian nations (Indonesia and the

Philippines, for example) has stepped up. That development could also help to bring the region's nations together in a common endeavor in combating other threats to their comprehensive security.

The U.S. and Asian expectations in 2003 that China will play a more proactive role in helping to defuse the North Korea nuclear buildup threat, with China's own interest in maintaining stability on the Korean peninsula,[110] are but two more incentives for the Chinese to step forward to become a stabilizing force in the region.

Developments since the Asian crisis have helped create a regional awareness that the countries, despite their diversities, share a common destiny in the face of the ravaging forces of globalization. The ASEAN's ten members are building a free trade area (FTA) with China known as the ASEAN+1 formula, cashing in on the vast Chinese market and the tumbling tariffs following China's entry into the World Trade Organization. Another factor drawing member nations closer together is that China has also begun to be seen as an intra-regional source of foreign direct investments (FDI) in these Asian neighbors. Both developments are extremely important because the ASEAN was originally conceived in the 1970s to promote member states' trade and security interests (China was then the threat). The rise of an ASEAN+1, as such, implies a strategic reconceptualization of the traditional security interests in today's changed world. It is also an indicator, however indirect, that ASEAN nations, like others, are now following a security dictate of a different sort, such as that of comprehensive security expounded previously in this paper.

ENDNOTES

[1] William T. Tow, "Introduction," in William T. Tow, Ramesh Thakur, and In-Taek Hyun, *Asia's Emerging Regional Order* (Tokyo and New York: United Nations University, 2000), pp. 1-10; James C. Hsiung, *Twenty-First Century World Order and the Asia Pacific* (New York: Palgrave, 2001), pp. 19; 26-34.

[2] "The Topicality of Comprehensive Security": Background paper for a Conference on Humanitarian Assistance & Comprehensive Security," 11 November 2003, at the University of Groningen, the Netherlands, p. 1.

[3] Olaf Palme Commission, *Common Security: A Blueprint for Survival* (New York: Simon & Schuster, 1982). Report of the Commission Disarmament and Security Issues.

[4] John Endicott, "Comprehensive Security: Politico-Military Aspects for a New Century," a paper presented to the Symposium: Towards Comprehensive Security in Asia, Tsukuba Advanced Research Alliance, Tsukuba Research City, Japan, 16 March 2001, p. 1. Obtainable from: Center for International Strategy, Technology, and Policy, Sam Nunn School of International Affairs, Georgia Institute of Technology, Atlanta, GA.

[5] U.S. Department of Defense, *The United States Security Strategy for the East Asia-Pacific Region* (Washington, D.C.: Department of Defense, November 1998).

[6] Cf. chapters by Davis Bobrow, Sueo Sudo, and Richard Hu, in Hsiung, *Twenty-First Century World Order.*

7   Steven Walt, "The Renaissance of Security Studies," *International Studies Quarterly*, Vol. 35, No. 2 (June 1991), pp. 211-239.

8   Ramesh Thakur, "From National to Human Security," in Stuart Harris and Andrew Mack, eds., *Asia Pacific Security: The Economic-Politics Nexus* (Sidney: Allen and Unwin, 1998), p. 53.

9   William T. Tow and Russell Trood, "Linkages Between Traditional Security and Human Security," in Tow, Thakur, and Hyun, eds., *Asia's Emerging Regional Order*, p. 15.

10 "Anarchical" does not mean chaos, but the lack of an overarching supranational authority over and above the sovereign states that constitute the Westphalian system we live in.

11 "Security dilemma" is a phenomenon that results from a competitive round of arms races kicked off when state X starts a hefty defense buildup to strengthen its own national security, provoking states Y, Z, and others to do a catch-up game out of fears of their own security being threatened. At time–n, however paradoxically, state X may find itself relatively less secure than at time–0, when it began its hefty defense buildup. In short, the concept of security dilemma, first developed by John Herz (1950) but reassessed in depth by Robert Jervis (1978) and Jack Snyder (1984), means that one state's security may incur another state's insecurity.

12 Barry Buzan, People, States, and Fear, 2d ed. (Boulder, CO: Lynne Rienner, 1991), p. 18.

13 As cited in Commission on Global Governance, *Our Global Neighborhood* (Oxford and New York: Oxford University Press, 1995), p. 80.

14 Cf. the International Human Development Program Research Project on Global Environmental Change and Human Security synopsis on "What is 'Human Security'?" on the Internet, available at <http://ibm.rhrz.uni-bonn.de/ihdp/gechs.htm>.

15 In this discussion, I shall rely largely on Hsiung, *Twenty-First Century World Order*, pp. 26–34 and 96–107, with necessary updating.

[16] Cf. James C. Hsiung, *Anarchy and Order: The Interplay of Politics and Law in International Relations* (Bouler, CO: Lynne Rienner, 1997), p. 203.

[17] Robert E. Hunter, "The United States in a New Era," in Brad Roberts, ed., *U.S. Foreign Policy After the Cold War* (Cambridge, MS: MIT Press, 1992), p. 9.

[18] Hsiung, *Twenty-First Century World Order*, p. 27.

[19] In 1995, for example, a trade war between the United States and Japan was averted at almost the last minute.

[20] Dennis Pirages, *Global Ecopolitics: The Context for International Relations* (North Scituate, MS: Duxbury Press), p. 5.

[21] For a discussion of global warming, for example, as an environmental issue that deserves attention on the international agenda, see James Sebenius, "Designing Negotiations Toward a New Regime: The Case of Global Warming," *International Security,* Vol. 15, No. 4 (Spring 1991), pp. 110-148.

[22] Lester R. Brown, "Challenges of the New Century," in Lester R. Brown, et al., eds., *State of the World 2000* (New York: W. W. Norton, 2000), pp. 5-6.

[23] "Europe Sizzles and Suffers in a Summer of Merciless Heat," *New York Times,* 6 August 2003, p. 3.

[24] Cited in Gareth Porter, "Environmental Security as a National Security Issue," *Current History* (May 1995), p. 221.

[25] UNDP, *Human Development Report 1993: Report of the United Nations Development Program* (New York: U.N. PIO, 1993). See discussion in UNA-USA, *A Global Agenda: Issues Before the 54th General Assembly of the United Nations* (Lanham, MD: Rowman & Littlefield, 1999).

[26] Thomas Weiss, et al., *The United Nations and Changing World Politics,* 2d ed. (Boulder, CO: Westview Press, 1997), p. 260.

[27] Lloyd Axworthy, "NATO's New Security Vocation," *NATO Review* (Winter, 1999), pp. 8-11.

[28] Michael Renner, *Fighting for Survival: Environmental Decline, Social Conflict, and the New Age of Insecurity* (New York: W.W. Norton, 1996), p. 81.

[29] Brown, et al., eds., *State of the World 2000,* pp. xviii; 4.

[30] Bates Gill and Sarah Palmer, "The Coming AIDS Crisis in China," *New York Times,* 16 July 2001, Op Ed page.

[31] Bjorn Lomberg, "The Environmentalists Are Wrong," *New York Times,* 26 August 2002, Op Ed page (p. 15).

[32] Trish Saywell, Geoffrey A. Fowler, and Shawn W. Crispin, "The Cost of SARS: $11 Billion and Rising," *Far Eastern Economic Review,* 24 April 2003, pp. 12-17.

[33] The eight are Japan, the "Four Tigers" (Korea, Taiwan, Hong Kong, and Singapore), China, and the three newly industrializing economies (NIEs) of Southeast Asia: Indonesia, Malaysia, and Thailand.

[34] World Bank, *The East Asian Miracle: Economic Growth and Public Policy* (Washington, D.C.: International Bank and Reconstruction & Development, 1993), pp. 2ff.

[35] E.g., Steffan Linder, *The Pacific Century: Economic and Political Consequences of Asia Pacific Dynamism* (Stanford, CA: Stanford University Press, 1986); William McCord, *The Dawn of the Pacific Century* (New Brunswick, N.J.: Transaction Publishers, 1991); Mark Borthwick, *The Pacific Century* (Boulder, CO: Westview Press, 1992); World Bank, *The East Asian Miracle* (1993).

[36] See n. 10 above for an explanation of "security dilemma."

[37] Jan Prybyla, "China and Taiwan: A Comparative Study of Economic Problems in the Asian Financial Crisis," *The American Asian Review,* Vol. 18, No. 4 (Winter 2000), pp. 69-114, at p. 70.

[38] Quoted in Hsiung, *Twenty-First Century World Order,* (p. 79).

[39] Criticisms of the IMF bail-out behavior during the crisis were widespread.

See Feldstein 1998, Calomiris 1998, and Vasquez 1998. Even the World Bank came out criticizing the IMF's response, which, among other things, made bank interest hikes a condition for IMF bailout to countries in trouble. The high-interest requirement caused many small and medium-sized companies to go bankrupt, making the economic meltdown worse. See discussion in Hsiung 2001 (p. 79 and n. 3).

40 Asian Development Bank, "Asian Recovery Report 2000," a semi-annual review of Asia's recovery from the crisis that began in July 1997. Available at: <http://aric.abd.org/external/arr2000/arr.htm>.

41 Tzong-shian Yu and Dianqing Xu, eds., *From Crisis to Recovery: East Asia Rising Again?* (Singapore: World Scientific, 2001), p. 25.

42 For a broader discussion of these lessons, see Hsiung, *Twenty-First Century World Order,* pp. 86-96.

43 Jonathan Lemco and Scott B. MacDonald, "Is Asian Financial Crisis Over?" *Current History,* Vol. 98, No. 632 (December 1999), pp. 433-437, at p. 434.

44 For a discussion of "contagion" in a currency crisis, see Takatoshi Ito, "Growth, Crisis, and the Future of Economic Recovery in East Asia," in Joseph E. Stiglitz and Shahid Yusuf, eds., *Rethinking the East Asian Miracle* (Oxford and New York: Oxford University Press, 2001), pp. 55-94, at p. 80; and Paul Krugman, *The Return of Depression Economics.* (New York, W.W. Norton, 2000), p. 96.

45 Takatoshi Ito's term, in Stigliz and Yusuf, eds., *Rethinking the East Asian Miracle,* p. 64.

46 Hsiung, *Twenty-First Century World Order,* pp. 84-85.

47 Robert Wade, "The Asian Crisis and the Global Economy: Causes, Consequences, and Cure," *Current History,* Vol. 97, No. 622 (November, 1998), pp. 361-373, at p. 367; World Bank, *East Asia: Recovery and Beyond* (Washington, D.C.: IBRD, 2000), pp. 32-33.

[48] Robert Wade, "The Asian Crisis," pp. 368-369.

[49] Douglas Sikorski, "The Financial Crisis in Southeast Asia and South Korea: Issues of Political Economy," *Global Economic Review* (Seoul), Vol. 28, No.1 (January, 1999), pp. 117-129, at p. 120.

[50] In a change of heart, the Korean government did allow more access to domestic markets by foreign banks and insurance companies, but at the same time required improvement in corporate and state disclosure to increase the transparency of the financial system, so as to upgrade the government's ability to control such matters as overborrowing, a crucial cause for Korea's succumbing to financial contagion. See Sikorski, *ibid.,* p. 120.

[51] Wade, "The Asian Crisis," p. 369.

[52] *Ibid.,* pp. 369-370.

[53] Hsiung, *Twenty-First Century World Order,* p. 87.

[54] Michael Porter, et al., *Can Japan Compete?* (Cambridge, MS: Perseus Publishing, 2000; and Gavan McCormack, *The Emptiness of Japanese Affluence,* rev. ed. (Armonk, NY: M.E. Sharpe, 2001).

[55] Sunday Owuala, "Banking Crisis Reforms, and the Availability of Credit to Japanese Small and Medium Enterprises," *Asian Survey,* Vol. 39, No. 4 (1999), pp. 656-667, at p. 667.

[56] When overborrowing from foreign monetary markets is controlled by heightened internal regulation, it obviates the problem known as casino effects of globalized capital (Hsiung 2001: 360–361).

[57] Paul Krugman, *Return of Depression Economics,* pp. 118ff.

[58] For a brief discussion of how these international currency speculators operate, see Krugman, *ibid.,* pp. 118-136.

[59] Hsiung, *Twenty-First Century World Order,* p. 90.

[60] Loksang Ho made a cogent plea on this point in a penetrating analysis of current crises, in Hsiung, ed., *ibid.,* p. 358.

61 James C. Hsiung, "The Aftermath of China's Accession to the WTO," *The Independent Review: A Journal of Political Economy,* Vol. 8, No. 1 (Summer, 2003), p. 100.

62 Cf. Sheldon Harris, *Factories of Death: Japanese Biological Warfare, 1932-45, and the American Cover-up* (New York and London: Routledge, 1994); Toshiyuki Tanaka and John W. Tower, *Hidden Horrors: Japanese War Crimes in World War II* (Boulder, CO: Westview Press, 1996); Iris Chang, *The Rape of Nanking: The Forgotten Holocaust of World War II* (New York: Basic Books, 1997).

63 See, for example, United Nations Development Program Report for 1998.

64 Hsiung, *Twenty-First Century World Order,* p. 101.

65 Samuel Lui, *Income Inequality and Economic Development* (Hong Kong: City University Press, 1997), p. 60, table 35.

66 Japan Insight 2000, "Population Aging and Longevity. Today's Japanese Men and Women Have the Longest Life Expectancy in the World," Data P-1. From: <http://www/jinjapan.org/insight/html>.

67 Masatishi Kanabayashi, "Immigration Attitudes Shift: Economic Realities May Force the Door Open," *Asian Wall Street Journal Weekly,* May 29-June 4, 2000, p. 10. Taking the 609,000 annual figure, and multiplying it by 50 years (2000-2050), I arrived at a total number of 30.5 million immigrants only. This is way below the 87.2 million working-age level in 1995 that Kanabayshi gave, citing the U.N. source. But, to be faithful to the original, I have kept his numbers.

68 Michael Antolik, *ASEAN and the Diplomacy of Accommodation* (Armonk, NY: M.E. Sharpe, 1990), pp. 11-12.

69 Lee Kuan Yew, *The Singapore Story: Memoirs of Lee Kuan Yew* (New York: Simon & Schuster, 1998).

70 Antolik, *ASEAN,* p. 29.

71 Final report of TGPF, sourced from <wysigwyg//31/http//www.geocities.com/Tokyo/Palace/2313/>.

72 CNN.com, at Web site <http://www.cnn.com/WORLD/asiapcf/9806/28/indenesia/apes/>.

73 A commentary on the dubious role played by the Indonesian army in these instances was found in "Jakarta Must Strike a Delicate Military Balance," by Barry Wain, in the *Asian Wall Street Journal Weekly,* June 26-July 2, 2000, p. 17.

74 Antolik, *ASEAN,* p. 30.

75 Alan Dupont, "Transnational Crime, Drugs, and Security in East Asia," *Asian Survey,* Vol. 39, No. 3 (1999), pp. 433-455.

76 *Ibid.,* p. 435, n.6.

77 Data from the Cabinet Office of Japan, International Labor Organization, and Inter-Parliamentary Union, as cited in "Japan's Neglected Resource: Female Workers," *New York Times,* 25 July 2003, p. 3.

78 Hsiung, *Twenty-First Century World Order,* p. 106.

79 Quoted in the same *New York Times* report, 25 July 2003, p. 3.

80 Anna Wu, "Hong Kong Should Have Equal Opportunities Legislation and a Human Rights Commission," in Michael Davis, ed., *Human Rights and Chinese Values* (London and New York: Oxford University Press, 1995), at p. 194.

81 According to the 1984 UK-China agreement on the return of Hong Kong, the "current system" (including the existing legal system) shall remain in place for fifty years. Cf. James C. Hsiung, *Hong Kong the Super Paradox* (New York: Palgrave, 2000), pp. 318-319.

82 AVISO Issue No. 1, 1998, p. 5. "Environmental Change, Vulnerability, and Security in the Pacific," online publication series of the Global

Environmental Change and Human Security, University of Michigan, Woodrow Wilson Center, and Canadian International Development Agency, at <http://www.gechs.org/aviso>.

83 J. Anthony, "Conflict over Natural Resources in the Pacific," In L. Ghee and M. Valencia, eds., *Conflict Over Natural Resources in South-East Asia and the Pacific* (New York: Oxford University Press, 1990).

84 An "archipelagic state" is defined in Article 46 of the 1982 Law of the Sea Convention as "a State constituted wholly by one or more archipelagos and may include other islands."

85 Brown, et al., *State of the World 2000,* p. 6.

86 Simon Elegant, "The Virus That Wouldn't Die," *Far Eastern Economic Review* (17 August 2000): pp. 16-17.

87 I treat sea lanes as a collective good shared by all East and Southeast Asian nations, as they are a vital "lifeline" in that they are indispensable to uninterrupted supply of badly-needed oil from the Middle East. For a discussion of these sea lanes in the context of military security, see Tun-hua Ko and Yu-ming Shaw, *Sea Lane Security in the Pacific Basin* (Taipei: Asia and the World Institute, 1983).

88 James C. Hsiung, "The Significance of Hu Jintao's Eurasia Visit, May 26-19, 2003," *Haixia pinlun* (Taipei), No. 151 (July 2003), at p.17.

89 James C. Hsiung, ed., *Asia Pacific in the New World Politics* (Boulder, CO: Lynne Rienner, 1993), pp. 15, 83.

90 Shee Poon Kim, "China's Changing Policies Toward the South China Sea," *The American Asian Review,* Vol. 12, No. 4 (Winter 1994), p. 67.

91 Peter Yu, "Issues on the South China Sea: A Case Study," in *Chinese Yearbook 1991-1992* (Taipei), pp. 138-200.

92 See discussion in Shee Poon Kim, "China's Changing Policies," p. 79.

93 Ludwig Schindler, "Fire Management in Indonesia—Quo Vadis?" sourced

from: http://www.iffin.or.id/itto.html; and IFFN No. 19, "Transboundary Haze Pollution in Southeast Asia," report by Daniel Murdiyarso, Program Head, BIOTROP-GCTE, Southeast Asia Impacts Center, Bogor, Indonesia, p. 3.

94 IFFM 2000, "Background on the Indonesian Fire Problem," information made available by the Indonesian Forest Fire Management office, at http://www.ifm.or.id/background.html.

95 "Indonesian Wildfires," report of the USCINCPAC Virtual Information Center, 20 March 2000, available at http://www.vic-info.org?RegionsTop.nsf/0/b4f66870b1821dff8a2568af00641.

96 "Indonesian Wildfires 2001," report of USCINCPAC Virtual Information Center, 11 July 2001: http://www/vic-info.org/RegionsTop.nsf/0/ea32c3a84a78ad678a256a8600805920/$FILE/Indonesian+Wildfires+07f11-01web.doc.

97 "Indonesian Wildfires Accelerated Global Warming," ENS dispatch, 8 November 2002. Results of the team's study were published in the November 7, 2002, issue of the journal *Nature*.

98 Paul Smith, "East Asia's Transnational Challenges: The Dark Side of Globalization," in Julian Weiss, ed., *Tigers' Roar: Asia's Recovery and Its Impact* (Armonk, NY: M.E. Sharpe, 2001), pp. 17-18.

99 See *Patterns of Global Terrorism, 1999.* U.S. Department of State publication 10687, released April 2000, www.state.gov/www/global/terrorism/1999report/appb.html.

100 See discussion in Smith, "East Asia' Transnational Challenges," p. 18.

101 *Ibid.,* p. 19.

102 Bertil Lintner, "The Perils of Rising Piracy," *Jane's Defense Weekly,* 34, 20: 16-17 (November 15, 2000).

103 Smith, "East Asia's Transnational Challenges," p. 20.

[104] Even Indonesia, the last country in the region to recover, decided not to renew the IMF bailout program initiated in 1997, when it expires at the end of 2003. *New York Times,* 30 July 2003: W1.

[105] *Qiaobao* [China Press] (New York), 18 April 2003, p. 2.

[106] Cf. Paul Smith, "East Asia's Transnational Challenges," pp. 15-17.

[107] Mikel Flamm, "Trafficking of Women and Children in Southeast Asia," *U.N. Chronicle,* Vol. 60, No. 2 (June 2003), pp. 34-36. Here, some 225,000 are transported across borders each year, according to U.S. State Department statistics, as compared to more than two million worldwide (at p. 34).

[108] Smith, "East Asia's Transnational Challenges," p. 20.

[109] Three examples of the Japanese atrocities during World War II include (a) Rape of Nanking, when 300,000 Chinese civilians were killed in a wanton three-week massacre by the Japanese Kwantung army, December 1937; (b) germ warfare; and (c) "Comfort Women," a practice in which hundreds of Asian women were abducted into Japanese military brothels to serve as sex slaves. See Chang, *Rape of Nanking*; Harris, *Factories of Death*; and Tanaka et al., *Hidden Horrors.*

[110] China's stakes in Korean peninsular stability emanates from the $42 billion annual trade that it has with South Korea. "China Breaks with Its Wartime Past," *Far Eastern Economic Review,* 7 April 2003, p. 25.

REFERENCES

Amsden, Alice H. 1989. *Asia's Next Giant: South Korea and Late Industrialization.* New York: Oxford University Press.

Anthony, J. 1990. "Conflict over Natural Resources in the Pacific," in *Conflict Over Natural Resources in South-East Asia and the Pacific,* eds., L. Ghee and M. Valencia. New York and Singapore: Oxford University Press.

Antolik, Michael. 1990. *ASEAN and the Diplomacy of Accommodation.* Armonk, NY: M.E. Sharpe.

Asian Development Bank. 2000. *Asian Recovery Report 2000,* a semiannual review of Asia's recovery from the crisis that began in July 1997. Available at <http://aric.adb.org/exteral/arr2000/arr.htm>.

AVISO Issue No. 1, 1998. Environmental Change, Vulnerability, and Security in the Pacific. Online publication series of the Global Environmental Change and Human Security Project, sponsored by the U.S. Agency for International Development, University of Michigan, Woodrow Wilson Center, and Canadian International Development Agency; available at: <http://www.gechs.org/aviso>.

Axworthy, Lloyd. 1999. "NATO's New Security Vocation," *NATO Review* (Winter), pp. 8-11.

Belassa, B., et al. 1982. *Developmental Strategies in Semi-Industrial Economies.* Baltimore, MD: Johns Hopkins University Press.

Berger, Peter, and Michael Hsiao, eds. 1986. *In Search of East Asian Developmental Model.* New Brunswick, NJ: Transaction Books.

Borthwick, Mark. 1992. *The Pacific Century.* Boulder, CO: Westview Press.

Brown, Lester R. 2000. "Challenges of the New Century," in *State of the World 2000,* eds., Lester Brown, Christopher Flavin, and Hilary French. *A*

Worldwatch Institute Report on Progress Toward a Sustainable Society. New York: W.W. Norton, pp. 3-21.

Buzan, Barry. 1991. *People, States, and Fear,* 2d ed. Boulder, CO: Lynne Rienner.

Calomiris, Charles W. 1998. "The IMF's Imprudent Role as Lender of Last Resort," *Cato Journal* 17,3.

Chang, Iris. 1997. *The Rape of Nanking: The Forgotten Holocaust of World War II.* New York: Basic Books.

CNN.com. 1998. "Reports Allege Organized Raping During Indonesian Riots," at Web site <http://www.cm.com/WORLD/asiapcf/9806/28/indonesia.apes/>.

Commission on Global Governance. 1995. *Our Global Neighborhood.* Oxford and New York: Oxford University Press.

Cummings, Bruce. 1987. "The Origins and Development of the Northeast Asian Political Economy: Industrial Sectors, Product Cycles, and Political Consequences," in *The Political Economy of the New Asian Industrialism,* ed., Frederick Deyo. Ithaca, NY: Cornell University Press.

Dower, John W. 1994. *Japan in Peace and War.* New York: New Press.

Dupont, Alan. 1999. "Transnational Crime, Drugs, and Security in East Asia." *Asian Survey,* 39, 3: 433-455.

Endicott, John. 2001. "Comprehensive Security: Politico-Military Aspects for a New Century," a paper presented to the Symposium: Towards Comprehensive Security in Asia, Tsukuba Advanced Research Alliance, Tsukuba Research City, Japan, 16 March 2001. Obtainable from: Center for International Strategy, Technology, and Policy, Sam Nunn School of International Affairs, Georgia Institute of Technology, Atlanta, GA.

Fei, John, Gustav Rainis, and Shirley Kuo. 1979. *Growth with Equity.* New York: Oxford University Press.

Feldstein, Mark. 1998. "The IMF's Errors," *Foreign Affairs* 77, 2: 20-33 (March/April).

Harris, Sheldon H. 1994. *Factories of Death: Japanese Biological Warfare, 1932-45, and the American Cover-up.* New York: Routledge.

Herz, John. 1950. "Idealist Internationalism," *World Politics,* 2, 2: 157-180.

Hofheinz, Roy, and Kent Calder. 1982. *The Eastasia Edge.* New York: Basic Books.

Hsiung, James C. 2003a. "The Aftermath of China's Accession to the World Trade Organization," *The Independent Review: A Journal of Political Economy* 8.1:87-112.

_____. 2003b. "The Significance of Hu Jintao's Eurasian Visit May 26-June 5, 20033," *Haixia pinglun* [Straits Review] (Taipei), No. 151 (July), pp. 16-19.

_____, ed. 2001. *Twenty-First Century World Order & the Asia Pacific.* New York: Palgrave-Macmillan.

_____, ed. 2000. *Hong Kong the Super Paradox: Life After Return to China.* New York: St Martin's Press.

_____. 1997. *Anarchy and Order: The Interplay of Politics and Law in International Relations.* Boulder, CO: Lynne Rienner.

_____, ed. 1993. *Asia Pacific in the New World Politics.* Boulder, CO: Lynne Rienner.

Hunter. Robert E. 1992. "The United States in a New Era," in *U.S. Foreign Policy After the Cold War,* ed., Brad Roberts. Cambridge, MS: MIT Press, 3-18.

IFFM. 2000. "Background on the Indonesian Fire Problem," information made available by the Indonesian Forest Fire Management, at <http://www.iffm.or.id/background.html>.

IFFN No. 19. "Transboundary Haze Pollution in Southeast Asia," report by Daniel Murdiyarso, Program Head, BIOTROP-GCTE, Southeast Asia Impacts Center, Bogor, Indonesia.

Japan Insight. 2000. "Population Aging and Longevity. Today Japanese Men and Women Have the Longest Life Expectancy in the World," sourced from Web site <http://www/jinjapan.org/insight/html>.

Jervis, Robert. 1978. "Cooperation Under the Security Dilemma," *World Politics,* 30, 2: 167-214 (January).

Kanabayashi, Masatishi. 2000. "Immigration Attitudes Shift: Economic Realities May Force the Door Open," *Asian Wall Street Journal Weekly* (May 29-June 4, 2000), p. 10. The U.N. projections cited are available in: Replacement Migration: Is It a Solution to Declining and Aging Populations? Available at Web site <wysiwyg//19//http://Russia.shaps.Hawaii.edu/>.

Keohane, Robert, and Joseph Nye. 1977. *Power and Interdependence.* Boston: Little, Brown.

Kim, Shee-Poon. 1994. See Shee, Poon Kim 1994, below.

Ko, Tun-hwa, and Yu-ming Shaw, eds. 1983. *Sea Lane Security in the Pacific Basin.* Taipei: Asia and the World Institute.

Krugman, Paul. 2000. *The Return of Depression Economics.* New York: W.W. Norton.

Lee, Kuan Yew. 1998. *The Singapore Story: Memoirs of Lee Kuan Yew.* New York: Simon and Schuster.

Lemco, Jonathan, and Scott B. MacDonald. 1999. "Is Asian Financial Crisis Over?' *Current History* 98, no. 632: 433-437 (December).

Linder, Steffan. 1986. *The Pacific Century: Economic and Political Consequences of Asia-Pacific Dynamism.* Stanford, CA: Stanford University Press.

Lui, Samuel Hon Kwong. 1997. *Income Inequality and Economic Development.* Hong Kong: City University Press.

McCord, William. 1991. *The Dawn of the Pacific Century: Implications for Three Worlds of Development.* New Brunswick, NJ: Transaction Publishers.

McCormack, Gavan. 2001. *The Emptiness of Japanese Affluence,* rev. ed. Armonk: NY: M.E. Sharpe.

Olaf Palme Commission. 1982. *Common Security: A Blueprint for Survival.* Report of the Commission on Disarmament and Security Issues. New York: Simon Schuster.

Owuala, Sunday. 1999. "Banking Crisis Reforms, and the Availability of Credit to Japanese Small and Medium Enterprises," *Asian Survey* 39, 4: 656-667.

Pirages, Dennis. 1978. *Global Ecopolitics: The New Context for International Relations.* North Scituate, MA: Duxbury Press.

Porter, Michael, Hirotaka Takeuchi, and Mariko Sakakibra. 2000. *Can Japan Compete?* Cambridge, MS: Perseus Publishing.

Prybyla, Jan S. 2000. "China and Taiwan: A Comparative Study of Economic Problems in the Asian Financial Crisis," *The American Asian Review* 18, 4: 69-114.

Rabushka, Alvin. 1987. *The New China.* Boulder, CO: Westview Press.

Renner, Michael. 1996. *Fighting for Survival: Environmental Decline, Social Conflict, and the New Age of Insecurity.* New York: W.W. Norton.

Schindler, Ludwig. 2000. "Fire Management in Indonesia—Quo Vadis?" Paper Given at the International Cross Sectoral Forum on Forest Fire Management in Southeast Asia, December 8-9, 1998, Jakarta. Available at <http://www.iffm.or.id/itto.html>.

Sebenius, James K. 1991. "Designing Negotiations Toward a New Regime: The Case of Global Warming," in *International Security,* 15, 4: 110-148 (Spring).

Shee, Poon Kim. 1994. "China's Changing Policies Toward the South China Sea," *The American Asian Review* 12, no. 4 (Winter).

Sikorski, Douglas. 1999. "The Financial Crisis in Southeast Asia and South Korea: Issues of Political Economy," *Global Economic Review* (Seoul) 28, 1: 117–129.

Smith, Paul. 2001. "East Asia's Transnational Challenges: The Dark Side of Globalization," in *Tigers' Roar: Asia's Recovery and Its Impact,* ed., Julian Weiss. Armonk, NY and London: M.E. Sharpe.

Snyder, Jack. 1984. "The Security Dilemma in Alliance Politics," *World Politics,* 36, 4: 461-496 (July).

Stiglitz, Joseph, and Shahid Yusuf, eds. 2001. *Rethinking the East Asian Miracle.* New York: Oxford University Press. A publication for the World Bank.

Tanaka, Toshiyuki, Yuki Tanaka, and John W. Tower. 1996. *Hidden Horrors: Japanese War Crimes in World War II.* Boulder, CO: Westview Press.

Thakur, Ramesh. 1998. "From National to Human Security," in *Asia-Pacific Security: The Economic-Politics Nexus,* eds., Stuart Harris and Andrew Mack. Sidney: Allen and Unwin.

Tow, William T., and Russell Trood. 2000. "Linkages Between Traditional Security and Human Security," in Tow, Thakur, and Hyun, eds. 2000.

Tow, William T., Ramesh Thakur, and In-Taek Hyun. 2000. *Asia's Emerging Regional Order: Reconciling Traditional and Human Security.* Tokyo, Paris, and New York: United Nations University Press.

UNA-USA 1999. *A Global Agenda: Issues Before the 54th General Assembly of the United Nations.* Lanham, MD: Rowman & Littlefield Publishers.

UNDP 1993. Human Development Report, issued by the United Nations Development Program, cited in UNA-USA 1999, p. 102.

Vasquez, Ian. 1998. Why the IMF Should Not Intervene? Summary of comments presented at the Conference on the Asian Crisis and the Reform of the Monetary System. Fundacion Dialogos. February 25, 1998. Madrid, Spain. Available at <http://www.Cato.org/speechew/sp-iv22598hml>.

Wade, Robert. 1998. "The Asian Crisis and the Global Economy: Causes, Consequences, and Cure," *Current History* 97, no. 622:361-373 (November).

Walt, Steven. 1991. "The Renaissance of Security Studies," *International Studies Quarterly,* 35, 2: 211-239 (June).

Weiss, Thomas, et al. 1997. *The United Nations and Changing World Politics,* 2d ed. Boulder, CO: Westview Press.

World Bank. 1993. *The East Asian Miracle: Economic Growth and Public Policy.* Washington, DC: International Bank of Reconstruction and Development.

_____. 2000. *East Asia: Recovery and Beyond.* Washington, DC: International Bank of Reconstruction and Development.

Wu, Anna. 1995. "Hong Kong Should Have Equal Opportunities Legislation and a Human Rights Commission," in *Human Rights and Chinese Values,* ed., Michael Davis. London and New York: Oxford University Press.

YRC (Yellow Ribbon Campaign). 1998. Final Report of the Joint Fact-Finding Team (TGPF). Sourced from: <wysiwyg://31/http://www.geocities.com/Tokyo/Palace/2313/>.

Yu, Peter. 1991-1992. "Issues on the South China Sea: A Case Study," in *Chinese Yearbook* (Taipei), 11:138-200.

Yu, Tzong-shian, and Dianqing Xu, eds. 2001. *From Crisis to Recovery: East Asia Rising Again?* Singapore and New Jersey: World Scientific.

ABOUT THE AUTHOR

James C. Hsiung is Professor of Politics at New York University, where he teaches international law, international-politics theory, and international governance. His teaching and research interests also include East Asian politics, Asian Pacific international relations, and Asian political culture. Among his broad professional concerns are America's strategic stakes in Asia Pacific. He is author and editor of 17 well-received books, including his *Twenty-First Century World Order and the Asia Pacific* (2001), *Anarchy and Order: The Interplay of Politics and Law in International Relations* (1997); and *Asia Pacific in the New World Politics* (1993).

During Hong Kong's crucial transition period of 1997–1999, Dr. Hsiung was Visiting Chair Professor and Head, Department of Politics and Sociology, Lingnan University. He observed, firsthand, the former British colony's return to China and completed an edited volume on various aspects of Hong Kong's changeover into a Chinese special administrative region (SAR). *Hong Kong the Super Paradox* (St. Martin's Press, 2000) claims to be the first such book in English bearing testimony to how the Hong Kong SAR managed to face off challenges to its viability and to make its unique "one country, two systems" model work under Chinese sovereignty.

Dr. Hsiung directs the Contemporary U.S.-Asia Research Institute, a New York-based think-tank, and is a former Executive Editor of *Asian Affairs,* a learned journal published in Washington, D.C. He holds the titles of Visiting Professor and Honorary Professor at a number of universities in China, including the Sun Yat-sen University (Canton) and Lingnan University in Hong Kong. A former consultant to the Singaporean Ministry of Education, Dr. Hsiung is a correspondent member of the Shanghai Academy of Social Sciences. His office address is Department of Politics, New York University, 726 Broadway, New York, NY 10003 USA. Tel.: (212) 998-8523. Fax: (212) 995-4184. E-mail: <jch2@nyu.edu>.

ABOUT THE
UNIVERSITY OF INDIANAPOLIS PRESS

The University of Indianapolis Press is a nonprofit publisher of original works, specializing in, though not limited to, topics with an international orientation. It is committed to disseminating research and information in pursuit of the goals of scholarship, teaching, and service. The Press aims to foster scholarship by publishing books and monographs by learned writers for the edification of readers. It supports teaching by providing instruction and practical experience through internships and practica in various facets of publishing, including editing, proofreading, production, design, marketing, and organizational management. In the spirit of the University's motto, "Education for Service," the Press encourages a service ethic in its people and its partnerships. The University of Indianapolis Press was institutionalized in August 2003; before its institutionalization, the University of Indianapolis Press published thirteen books, eight of which were under the auspices of the Asian Programs. The Press had specialized in Asian Studies and, as part of its commitment to support projects with an international orientation, will continue to focus on this field while encouraging submission of manuscripts in other fields of study.

BOOKS FROM THE
UNIVERSITY OF INDIANAPOLIS PRESS

(1992–2003)

1. Phylis Lan Lin, Winston Y. Chao, Terri L. Johnson, Joan Persell, and Alfred Tsang, eds. (1992) *Families: East and West.*

2. Wei Wou (1993) *KMT-CCP Paradox: Guiding a Market Economy in China.*

3. John Langdon and Mary McGann. (1993) *The Natural History of Paradigms.*

4. Yu-ning Li, ed. (1994) *Images of Women in Chinese Literature.*

5. Phylis Lan Lin, Ko-Wang Mei, and Huai-chen Peng, eds. (1994) *Marriage and the Family in Chinese Societies: Selected Readings.*

6. Phylis Lan Lin and Wen-hui Tsai, eds. (1995) *Selected Readings on Marriage and the Family: A Global Perspective.*

7. Charles Guthrie, Dan Briere, and Mary Moore. (1995) *The Indianapolis Hispanic Community.*

8. Terry Kent and Marshall Bruce Gentry, eds. (1996) *The Practice and Theory of Ethics.*

9. Phylis Lan Lin and Christi Lan Lin. (1996) *Stories of Chinese Children's Hats: Symbolism and Folklore.*

10. Phylis Lan Lin and David Decker, eds. (1997) *China in Transition: Selected Essays.*

11. Phylis Lan Lin, ed. (1998) *Islam in America: Images and Challenges.*

12. Michelle Stoneburner and Billy Catchings. (1999) *The Meaning of Being Human.*

13. Frederick D. Hill. (2003) *'Downright Devotion to the Cause': A History of the University of Indianapolis and Its Legacy of Service.*

For information on the above titles or to place an order, contact:
University of Indianapolis Press
1400 East Hanna Avenue / Indianapolis, IN 46227 USA
(317) 788-3288 / (317) 788-3480 (fax)
lin@uindy.edu / http://www.uindy.edu/universitypress

NEW TITLES FROM THE
UNIVERSITY OF INDIANAPOLIS PRESS

(2004–2005)

1. brenda Lin. *Wealth Ribbon: Taiwan Bound, America Bound.*

2. May-lee Chai. *Glamorous Asians: Short Stories and Essays.*

3. Chiara Betta. *The Other Middle Kingdom: A Brief History of Muslims in China* (in Chinese and English). Translated by Phylis Lan Lin and Cheng Fang.

4. Phylis Lan Lin and Cheng Fang. *Operational Flexibility: A Study of the Conceptualizations of Aging and Retirement in China* (in Chinese and English). Translated by Phylis Lan Lin and Cheng Fang.

5. Alyia Ma Lynn. *Muslims in China* (in Chinese and English). Translated by Phylis Lan Lin and Cheng Fang.

6. Philip H. Young. *In Days of Knights: A Story for Young People.*

7. James C. Hsiung. *Comprehensive Security: Challenge for Pacific Asia.*

8. Winberg Chai. *Saudi Arabia: A Modern Reader.*

9. Au Ho-nien. *Journey with Art Afar.* Catalog for the Au Ho-nien Museum, University of Indianapolis.

Wealth Ribbon: Taiwan Bound, America Bound
Essays

By brenda Lin

Wealth Ribbon: Taiwan Bound, America Bound is a thematic narrative that intertwines the coming-of-age story of Taiwan with three generations of the author's family history and relationship with American culture. Together, these interconnected essays form a distinctive view of what it is like to have a transnational identity and show how the everyday politics of an international cultural identity is in fact quite universal.

"Language" focuses on Lin's grandmother, who grew up in Taiwan during the Japanese occupation speaking Japanese fluently and developing a strong cultural tie to Japan. The story shows how language played an important part in defining what it meant to be Taiwanese in the post-occupation era, when Taiwan was returned to China. "Place" traces the story of Lin's father, whom she uses as a symbol for the new Taiwanese identity of his generation— opportunistic and entrepreneurial people who immigrated to the United States in the 1970s only to return home after just a few years, despite Taiwan's uncertain political future. "Nationality" describes Lin's first trip to mainland China, where she becomes conscious of her displacement traveling as a Taiwanese-American on the mainland, which raises poignant questions about national identity and cultural loyalty. In the last three chapters—"Home," "Translations," and "Umbilical Cord"—the three generations of Lin's family, which represent both similar and different languages and cultures, come together in a sometimes cacophonous, other times melodious, symphony of emotions. This collection of narrative essays weaves together a ribbon of unique experiences that readers of all backgrounds will be able to relate to.

"The Taiwanese were one of the first major groups of Asians to come to America in large numbers after the 1965 Civil Rights Act changed immigration laws, yet little has been written about their culture and experiences.

"This moving memoir of a Taiwanese-American family is both lyrical and intelligent, filled with humor, insight, and poignancy. *Wealth Ribbon* is a rare treasure indeed." —May-lee Chai, author of *The Girl from Purple Mountain* and *My Lucky Face*

"Naming oneself would seem to be the easiest task in the world, but brenda Lin teaches us that naming our national identity is just the beginning, while 'becoming' something, such as an American, is quite another story. What a fascinating journey." —Shawn Wong, author of *Homebase* and *American Knees*

brenda Lin received her M.F.A. from Columbia University. Her essays have appeared in *Fourth Genre, Mr. Beller's Neighborhood,* and *Full Circle Journal.* She has cowritten a book with her mother and grandmother (*Bonding via Baby Carriers,* Les Enphants, 2001). Currently, she lives in New York City, where she is working on her second book.

University of Indianapolis Press

List Price: US $16.95
For book orders,
please contact the
University of Indianapolis Press
1400 East Hanna Avenue
Indianapolis, Indiana 46227
lin@uindy.edu
(317) 788-3480 (fax)

Glamorous Asians
Short Stories and Essays

By May-lee Chai

In this lyrical collection, May-lee Chai explores the diversity of the Asian-American experience, challenging stereotypes while experimenting with form, language, metaphor, and myth.

For example, in "The Dancing Girl's Story," a goddess fleeing the civil war in Cambodia is picked up by a Coast Guard ship and interrogated by uncomprehending INS officials. In "Nai-nai's Last Words," a son ponders the meaning of his mother's ghostly appearance after her death. In "Easter," the biracial children of a Nebraska farmer and his Filipina showgirl wife must cope with the loss of their mother as well as their father's way of life in their small farming community. In her title essay, "Glamorous Asians," Chai combines family stories with musings about the nature of cultural representation and images of beauty in America for a witty send-up of the American glamour industry. Her final essay explores, with humor and insight, continuing notions of "Yellow Peril" amidst political scapegoating as well as images of Chinese-Americans as eternal foreigners in their own country.

Together, these stories and essays provide a unique portrait of a diverse world.

"I laughed and cried aloud as I read *Glamorous Asians*. May-lee Chai is a gifted young writer whose scalpel-sharp wit cuts through the heart of immigrant America. In this wonderful new addition to Asian-American literature, Chai explores the mysteries—and brutal realities—of invisible lives, of people misunderstood or simply ignored by mainstream culture, by giving voice to their unfulfilled dreams, secret ambitions, and hidden triumphs. This collection sings with despair, rage, exhaustion—and hope."—Iris Chang, *New York Times'* bestselling author of *The Rape of Nanking* and *The Chinese in America*.

"The beauty of this slim, evocative collection lies not only in the highly personalized portraits of Asian Americans, but also in May-lee Chai's gracefully nuanced writing. It is a small treasure." —Howard Goldblatt, professor of Chinese, University of Notre Dame.

"Full of wonderment, *Glamorous Asians* elucidates the innermost feelings and thoughts of Asian Americans who are not afraid of exhibiting their own agency and empowerment as they navigate through civil wars, death, a farmer's life, immortality, marriage, history, and racism—and of being glamorous. This is a notably artistic achievement for May-lee Chai." —Anthony B. Chan, associate professor, Communication and International Studies, University of Washington.

"*Glamorous Asians* rises above the froth of mass marketing chic. In this book, May-lee Chai renders the folly and wisdom of youth and age and lays bare the heartbreak beneath gender, culture, and class. We're in the hands of a sophisticate with a piercing eye, a nuanced intelligence, and a sprightly sense of irony."—Marilyn Krysl, author of *Warscape with Lovers* and *How to Accommodate Men: Short Stories*.

May-lee Chai is the author of a novel, *My Lucky Face* (NY: Soho, 1997), and coauthor with her father of a family memoir, *The Girl from Purple Mountain* (NY: St. Martin's Press, 2001), which was nominated for the National Book Award. She is a former reporter for the Associated Press and has taught creative writing at the University of Colorado-Boulder and San Francisco State University. May-lee Chai graduated from Grinnell College with a B.A. degree in French and Chinese Studies. She received a master's degree in East Asian Studies from Yale University and a master's in English-Creative Writing from the University of Colorado. Beginning this fall, she will be teaching creative writing at Amherst College in Massachusetts.

University of Indianapolis Press

List Price: US $16.95
ISBN 0-880938-57-9
For book orders,
please contact the
University of Indianapolis Press
1400 East Hanna Avenue
Indianapolis, Indiana 46227
lin@uindy.edu
(317) 788-3480 (fax)

The Other Middle Kingdom:
A Brief History of Muslims in China

By Chiara Betta

Translated by Phylis Lan Lin and Cheng Fang

(in English and Chinese)

The history of Muslims in China spans more than fourteen centuries and cannot be exhaustively analyzed in a single work. Notwithstanding the inevitable limitations of space, *The Other Middle Kingdom* will attempt to present this often-overlooked chapter of Chinese history, which has been revalued by scholars from various academic disciplines only in recent years. The main aim of this study is to challenge the widespread stereotype of China as a highly homogenous country. Westerners not well acquainted with Chinese cultural heritage often consider China as monolithic nation where everyone speaks the same language, eats rice, and shares similar, if not identical, cultural practices. This perception is distorted, given the fact that China is characterized by enormous cultural and linguistic differences among even the Han Chinese nationality (*minzu*) (Gladney, 1998).

This study is in two parts. The first touches on early Muslim life in China and highlights the fact that Muslims underwent a process of cross-cultural adaptation in the host environment from the Yuan period onward. It also discusses the 1759 conquest of the central Asian region of Xinjiang, which brought a large population of Turkic Muslims under control of the Qing Empire. The second discusses the twentieth century, dissecting the ten Muslim nationalities recognized by the People's Republic of China (PRC).

Chiara Betta completed her first degree in Oriental Languages and Literature at the University of Venice in Italy in 1990 after studying Chinese and Chinese history at Beijing University for two years with a scholarship provided by the Italian Ministry of Foreign Affairs. In 1997, she was awarded a PhD in modern Chinese history at the School of Oriental and African Studies, University of London. Professor Betta's research interests concentrate on Shanghai's social history and the trade diasporas of Baghdadi Jews in the nineteenth and twentieth centuries. With the encouragement of Dr. Phylis Lan Lin of the University of Indianapolis, Professor Betta has recently started to research the history of Islam in China and the question of ethnic nationalism in Chinese Central Asia.

Professor Betta has presented papers at international conferences in the United States, China, Italy, France, Great Britain, Germany, Portugal, Israel, and Greece. Her recent publications include the contribution of chapters in the volumes *The Jews of China: Historical and Comparative Perspectives* (edited by Jonathan Goldstein) and *New Frontiers: Imperialism's New Communities in East Asia, 1842-1952* (edited by Robert Bickers and Christian Henriot).

Professor Betta is writing a book entitled *Tycoon: Silas Hardoon in Old and New Shanghai, 1874-1997,* which is based on her PhD and dissertation. Dr. Betta has been teaching at the University of Indianapolis-Athens since 1999.

**University of
Indianapolis Press**

List Price: US $19.95
For book orders,
please contact the
University of Indianapolis Press
1400 East Hanna Avenue
Indianapolis, Indiana 46227
lin@uindy.edu
(317) 788-3480 (fax)

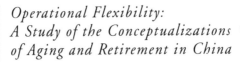

Operational Flexibility: A Study of the Conceptualizations of Aging and Retirement in China

By Phylis Lan Lin and Cheng Fang

(in English and Chinese)

With the implementation of an open-door reform policy, and accelerating industrialization, China is witnessing a momentous demographic shift. This social restructuring of the population, characterized by the rapid aging of its citizens, will lead to a variety of urgent problems, among which aging and retirement remain at the core. China is different from the West in that it is not what sociologists call "an employee society"; thus, aging does not necessarily mean retirement, and vice versa. This problem appears to be more complicated. It is often determined by the economic conditions and authoritative operational flexibility that underwrite the ideologies of convention and power.

China is a politically hierarchical, economically polarized, and culturally diverse society. For this social actuality, this monograph explores various conceptualizations of aging and retirement in China based on the hierarchical social status imposed by arbitrary political power. This monograph discusses five aspects of aging and retirement: types of aging groups and the conceptualizations of retirement, eligibility for retirement and its implications, operational flexibility and patterns of retirement, differences in pension and social welfare, and issues of retirement and their impact on research about aging.

This monograph concludes that aging and retirement are two relatively independent concepts in China. The majority of China's population is not yet eligible for retirement, and those who benefit from the retirement privileges are granted diverse pension incomes and social welfare. This monograph is part of the global aging project cosponsored by the University of Indianapolis Center for Aging and Community and the University's Asian Programs.

Phylis Lan Lin is a professor of Sociology at the University of Indianapolis and the director of the University's Graduate Applied Sociology Program, the director of Asian Programs, the president's international ambassador, and executive director of the University of Indianapolis Press. Professor Lin received her Ph.D. in Sociology from the University of Missouri-Columbia in 1972. She has organized and chaired numerous international conferences. In gratitude for Dr. Lin's founding of the Social Work Program at the University of Indianapolis, the program was named the "Phylis Lan Lin Program in Social Work" on April 2, 1997. Dr. Lin was selected as one of the 33 most influential women in Indiana by the *Indianapolis Business Journal* in 2002. Dr. Lin has written and edited more than fifteen books in both Chinese and English.

Cheng Fang is now a full-time professor and doctoral supervisor of Nanjing University, teaching English and American Literature, Modern and Contemporary Critical Theories, and History of European Civilizations. He received his B.A. in English from Shaanxi Normal University in 1985, his M.A. in English and American Literature from Sichuan University in 1993, and his Ph.D. in American Literature from Nanjing University in 1998.

University of Indianapolis Press

List Price: US $12.95
For book orders,
please contact the
University of Indianapolis Press
1400 East Hanna Avenue
Indianapolis, Indiana 46227
lin@uindy.edu
(317) 788-3480 (fax)

Muslims in China

By Aliya Ma Lynn

Translated by Phylis Lan Lin and Cheng Fang
(in English and Chinese)

"How awkward I feel when people ask, 'Are there Muslims in China?' There is so much to tell and let the world know about Muslims in China, but there is such scant literature, in English especially, to transmit the information.

"I am a Chinese Muslim, I grew up in a Muslim family, and I married a Muslim scholar. I made a special trip to China in 2000 and toured four northwestern provinces. My scholarly friends offered me books, magazines, and journals to quench my thirst for information. They helped me present a more complete picture of Muslims in China in both the past and the present." —Aliya Ma Lynn

Aiya Ma Lynn, or Mrs. Shums Tung Tao Chang, is originally from Beijing. She attended the American University of Cairo in Cairo, Egypt. As a journalism major, she also attended Fu Tan University (1946-1949) in Shanghai, China. From 1950 to 1970, she serviced as a news translator and announcer in Broadcasting Services, Singapore, and later became a media producer in Radio and TV Malaysia. From 1970 to 1977, she lectured on Chinese language and literature at Nanyang University of Singapore.

Now a freelance writer, she is a member, former president (1966-1998), and president-elect (2004–2006) of the National League of American Pen Women (NLAPW, Phoenix Branch), Phoenix Writer's Club, Arizona State, and the Phoenix Branch Poetry Association. Many of her poems, prose, and travelogues were published in both English and Chinese magazines in Hong Kong, Malaysia, Singapore, Taiwan, and China.

**University of
Indianapolis Press**

List Price: US $19.95
For book orders,
please contact the
University of Indianapolis Press
1400 East Hanna Avenue
Indianapolis, Indiana 46227
lin@uindy.edu
(317) 788-3480 (fax)

In Days of Knights

By Philip H. Young

Into the mysterious world of King Arthyr—a time of magic, knights, ladies, and the quest for goodness and for the Holy Grail—enters an ordinary boy named Cedrych from the little village of Dornbridge. Through a series of unlikely events, he learns about knighthood and dreams of going to the great city of Camelot. His courage and good character serve him well as squire to Sir Gawain, who must fight the dreaded Green Knight, and for his service King Arthyr makes him a Knight of the Round Table! Many adventures follow, as Sir Cedrych joins the other knights in their quests to do good deeds throughout the kingdom. Will they be able to solve a puzzle that will save the king and queen? . . . outsmart a dangerous dragon who is ravaging a village? . . . find the maiden who controls a unicorn? . . . and even find the Holy Grail?

Through it all, Sir Cedrych never forgets his humble roots and, especially, his boyhood sweetheart, a pretty girl named Maralynne. He and his best friend, Sir Parsivale, both keep faith with lovers from their past, hoping against hope to meet them once again. Suddenly, everything at Camelot changes, as the mystical Holy Grail appears, the sorcerer Myrddin brings the Perfect Knight to the Round Table, and evil begins to work its way through the chinks in the fortifications of the righteous kingdom. As the fate of Logres draws nearer and nearer to disaster, will the genial, down-to-earth Cedrych be able to survive, and will he ever see his first love again? And what will become of this realm of goodness and civilization if King Arthyr himself should be betrayed and killed?

This novel is written especially for young people, ages 12 to adult.

University of Indianapolis Press

List Price: US $17.95
For book orders,
please contact the
University of Indianapolis Press
1400 East Hanna Avenue
Indianapolis, Indiana 46227
lin@uindy.edu
(317) 788-3480 (fax)

Philip H. Young is the director of Krannert Memorial Library at the University of Indianapolis. In addition to a master's degree in Library and Information Science, he holds a Ph.D. in Classical Archaeology. Although he has published scholarly books and articles, this is his first novel.

Comprehensive Security: Challenge for Pacific Asia

By James C. Hsiung

Security studies in the twenty-first century entail a paradigm shift from the traditional concerns of national defense (military security) to other dimensions, namely the economic, environmental, and human security of nations. After September 11, the traditional notion of security takes on an anti-terrorist connotation, giving a new salience to "homeland security."

This study, by Dr. James C. Hsiung of New York University, is a coherent explication of comprehensive security in the above-named dimensions. It compares the conceptual implications of comprehensive security with those of both traditional security and its post-9/11 anti-terror variant, then turns to an in-depth discourse on the meanings of each of the three dimensions of comprehensive security as experienced in Pacific Asia.

Findings from the region's experience have wider inferential value in other parts of the world. For example, the economic, environmental, and human dimensions of security are closely intertwined, as shown in the recent SARS attack. The virus's spread underscored a source of environmental insecurity and posed a challenge to human security (as hundreds of individuals succumbed to the virus), with an estimated $5-billion impact on the region's economic security. This recalls the AIDS scourge or other epidemics in other regions that affected economic, environmental, and human security dimensions.

Another finding with wider relevance is that the tasks of protecting a nation's comprehensive security today—such as in combating global warming (i.e., threats to environmental security), no less than in fighting the ravaging "casino effects" of globalized capital (a threat to economic security) or global terrorism (a threat to human security)—require multinational collaboration. The bottom line is that no nation's self-help will be adequate for comprehensive security—not even a hyperpower like the United States, as September 11 and the subsequent global anti-terror campaign amply demonstrate.

Dr. James C. Hsiung is Professor of Politics at New York University, where he teaches international law, international-politics theory, and international governance. His teaching and research interests include East Asian politics, Asian Pacific international relations, and Asian political culture. Among his interests are America's strategic stakes in Asia Pacific. He is author and editor of 17 well-received books, including his *Twenty-First Century World Order and the Asia Pacific* (2001), *Anarchy and Order: The Interplay of Politics and Law in International Relations* (1997); and *Asia Pacific in the New World Politics* (1993).

During Hong Kong's crucial transition period of 1997–1999, Dr. Hsiung was visiting Chair Professor and Head, Department of Politics and Sociology, at Lingnan University. He observed firsthand the former British colony's return to China and completed an edited volume on various aspects of Hong Kong's change to a Chinese special administrative region (SAR). *Hong Kong the Super Paradox* (St. Martin's Press, 2000) claims to be the first such book in English bearing testimony to how the Hong Kong SAR managed to face challenges to its viability and to make its unique "one country, two systems" model work under Chinese sovereignty.

Born in mainland China and a graduate of National Taiwan University, he immigrated to America in 1958. He received his Ph.D. from Columbia University, where he also taught. He is one of a very few Chinese-American academics who enjoy rapport with top Chinese leaders as well as academics in both Beijing and Taipei. He had a six-hour audience with Deng Xiaoping, China's ultimate leader, in 1987. He is a former advisor to the Singaporean government on educational policy. His community-affairs credentials include advisory affiliations with a number of Chinese-American civic, business, and banking organizations (e.g., Chinese Import and Export Association of America, Jiangxi Landsmanschaft, Friends of Hong Kong and Macao Committee). He is a cofounder of the Chinese American Academic and Professional Society in New York. He doubles as an occasional consultant to businesses in Taiwan, Hong Kong, and China proper.

Dr. Hsiung directs the Contemporary U.S.-Asia Research Institute, a New York-based think tank, and is a former executive editor of *Asian Affairs,* a learned journal published in Washington, D.C. He holds the title of Visiting Professor or Honorary Professor at a number of universities in China, including the Sun Yat-sen University (Canton), and at Lingnan University in Hong Kong. He is a consultant member of the Shanghai Academy of Social Sciences.

University of Indianapolis Press

List Price: US $16.95
For book orders,
please contact the
University of Indianapolis Press
1400 East Hanna Avenue
Indianapolis, Indiana 46227
lin@uindy.edu
(317) 788-3480 (fax)

Saudi Arabia: A Modern Reader

Edited by Winberg Chai, Ph.D., D.H.L., D.L.

Although many recent polemical books have been written, either criticizing the Saudi Kingdom and its relationship with the United States or praising the Kingdom for allying with the United States, none has tried to provide nonpartisan, up-to-date, and basic information about this important nation and its complicated relationship with the United States.

Saudi Arabia: A Modern Reader aims to fill this gap by providing readers with enough background, historical data, and contemporary information about the Kingdom of Saudi Arabia to provide American citizens and other English readers with the fundamental information they need in order to understand Saudi Arabia's key role in the Middle East and to form their own opinions about its present and future relationship to the United States.

The book's editor, political scientist Dr. Winberg Chai, provides in his introduction a concise overview of this largely unknown Kingdom for American readers, from its geography and history to its contemporary role in the "war on terrorism." He then selects important documents, journalists' articles, political leaders' public statements, and academic essays that illuminate the unique character, development, modernization, and contemporary troubles facing the Kingdom of Saudi Arabia. The editor's criteria for selection have been relevance and readability. The editor has tried not to abridge selections, in order to maintain the sense of the original.

The *Reader* is divided into four parts: US-Saudi Relations; Saudi Arabian Modernization; War Against Terrorism; and Current Background and Statistics. It also includes a useful appendix and glossary that will help readers readily access definitions of terms they may not be familiar with. This *Reader* offers a fascinating and illuminating portrait of the powerful forces of continuity as well as change in this important country, an essential United States ally in the Middle East today.

Dr. Winberg Chai is a professor of political science at the University of Wyoming. He is the author and editor of more than twenty books. Dr. Chai has traveled extensively in the Middle East, including frequent visits to Saudi Arabia over the course of more than three decades. He currently serves as Executive Editor of *Asian Affairs: An American Review,* a scholarly journal published by Heldref Publications of Washington, D.C.

University of Indianapolis Press

For book orders, please contact the
University of Indianapolis Press
1400 East Hanna Avenue
Indianapolis, Indiana 46227
lin@uindy.edu
(317) 788-3480 (fax)

Journey with Art Afar
The Au Ho-nien Museum

University of Indianapolis

Translations of Chinese painting inscriptions
by Bonnie Kwan Huo

(in English and Chinese)

The University of Indianapolis and its Asian Programs initiative are proud to announce the Au Ho-nien Museum in the Schwitzer Student Center. The Center serves as the vibrant heart of campus life, and the Museum's presence in this facility will ensure maximum visibility of the works of this world-renowned artist. Students, faculty, staff, campus visitors, and community members will be able to view this collection free of charge, reinforcing the University's commitment to promoting awareness of cultural diversity. A painter, poet, calligrapher, scholar, and teacher, Master Au is committed to communicating the aesthetic values of the traditional Chinese masters, and his art is informed by that long cultural history. It is a testament to the stunning quality and execution of his work that the subject matter and themes, though often thoroughly Chinese, are instantaneously translatable to viewers worldwide, in effect bridging East and West. "We've been most fortunate over the years," says Jerry Israel, University president, "to introduce this consummate artist to our campus and the community; his paintings have graced the walls of our Christel DeHaan Fine Arts Center gallery for several special exhibitions. His elegant triptych 'Seven Sages of the Bamboo Groves' covers the greater part of one wall in my own office, and it is a visual oasis in an often hectic schedule. I know full well the power of his work."

Master Au Ho-nien, born in 1935 in China's southern province of Kwangtung, is today widely recognized as a leading contemporary artist in Chinese painting. He is Hwakang Professor of Art at the Chinese Culture University at Yangming Shan, Taipei, a prestigious post—Taiwan's highest accolade for an artist. Master Au promotes the aesthetic traditions of Chinese culture through his numerous exhibitions and educational presentations. Since 1956, he has been invited to give one-man and joint art exhibits in some of the world's leading galleries and museums, including the National Museum of the Republic of China, Taiwan; the Tokyo Central Museum of Art, Japan; Museum fur Kunsthandwerk, Germany; and the Musee Cernushi in France. Master Au's paintings have been collected by numerous museums around the world, including the British Museum in England; the San Diego Museum and the Asian Art Museum of San Francisco in the U.S.; the Hong Kong Heritage Museum in Hong Kong; the Taiwan Museum of Art in Taiwan; the Musee Cernuschi in France; and the National Chinese Museum in Beijing, China. Master Au became a fellow of the Chinese Academy in 1968 and Academician of the Chinese Academy in 1974. He received an honorary doctor of philosophy degree from the Wonkwang University, Korea, in 1994 and an honorary doctor of arts degree from the University of Indianapolis in 1995. He has received the Global Overseas Chinese Culture Award, the Golden Goblet Award of Chinese Art from the Chinese Art Association, and the International Communication Service Award from the Government Information Office in Taiwan, and participated with honors in the French National Society of Fine Arts Biennial Exhibition at the Grand Palais Museum of Paris.

University of Indianapolis Press

List Price: US $35.00
For book orders,
please contact the
University of Indianapolis Press
1400 East Hanna Avenue
Indianapolis, Indiana 46227
lin@uindy.edu
(317) 788-3480 (fax)

INDEX